PASSIVE INCOME IDEAS

Make money Online Trought Dropshipping,
Affiliate Marketing, Instagram Marketing, Influencer
Marketing, Ecommerce, Amazon FBA,
Self-Publishing and much more

Jonathan Becker

TABLE OF CONTENTS

INTRODUCTION

No one needs to work 40 or more hours seven days for long. If you do you're insane. If you don't, you better start learning a few things about passive income. It's the retirement plan of intelligent people. In case you maintain a business or need to keep a company, with the end goal to have the opportunity in life you long for you need to start thinking of some passive income ideas to enable you to earn increasingly and work less.

It is an incredible inclination when you can require some serious energy off at whatever point you need to, without stressing over what will happen to your business.

As a business person, there is always going to be a limit on the amount you can earn except if you can make money without being specifically engaged with the work. You're not rich except if you can make money in your rest.

Passive income ideas enable a business visionary to earn income without requiring your immediate contribution — for instance; sovereignties on an innovative piece (music, book, creation and so forth), owning property, offers, and network marketing.

There are numerous ways to earn a passive income,

some less demanding than others. The most outstanding ways are to purchase a venture property or put resources into offers yet these expect you to have the money in any case. The best passive income ideas are the ones that require little startup expenses however still offer to compensate compensation whenever executed well.

There is no denying we are in the age of the web and all things considered there are numerous open doors online to earn a passive income. Activities like Google AdSense enable people to receive money from making prominent content. There are additionally many affiliate programs that will allow you to earn a rate when people click through from your site and purchase an item; Amazon is notable for this. If you can make content online that people need to see, there are numerous ways to make a benefit out of it.

At that point there is network marketing, there are a large number of old and new network marketing organizations going back and forth constantly. Customarily, the trick shame has always been appended to network marketing and sometimes in light of current circumstances, however, there are numerous legitimate organizations engaged with this kind of marketing nowadays, and there is some genuine money to be made for people that can do it well.

We have just talked around a couple of the passive income ideas that are out there; there are a large number of ways to earn the remaining income. It might originate from rehashed deals or new clients, and it might require a tad bit of your time or zero however the key is that you are making money off of other people's work or no work, instead of by your own.

Applying It

There is no time like the present to start thinking about how to incorporate this kind of thinking in your business. You have to ask yourself; would you be able to make an item that people will purchase again and again? Would you be able to connect with others to offer your piece? How might you make money off crafted by others?

The sooner you answer these inquiries, the sooner you'll have money related and individual flexibility. Start thinking about some passive income ideas that will enable your business to wind up less time expanding and start living your fantasies while you keep on earning income.

CHAPTER ONE

THINK ABOUT THE PASSIVE INCOME IDEAS TO MAKE MONEY ONLINE

Numerous people think about whether there are passive income ideas accessible which could transform a customary blog into a genuine way to make money. Shockingly, the appropriate response is yes - a vast number of bloggers are getting some answers concerning the passive income streams they could be utilizing further bolstering their advantage. Loads of people have gotten on board the temporary blogging fad. Who wouldn't like to wind up a distributed author with many faithful fans?

When we discovered that writing business or individual weblogs could make us money, we as a whole needed to get in on it. A couple of passive income ideas, a great blog (and they exist on about each subject), and the adoration for writing can be genuine benefit makers. Passive income streams are wherever for people who realize how to utilize them legitimately.

In any case, the world is loaded with scholars who aren't profiting. The clients are making the most and utilizing their income ideas minus all potential limitations are energetic about what they do. Nobody needs to peruse content that even the essayist had no enthusiasm for. An extremely devoted after of all around pointed guests is essential to make the large portion of the income streams accessible. Nobody ought to overlook that the readers are the place the money originates from. Disregarding the readers implies losing the possibility at a decent benefit.

The clients destined to bomb, regardless of whether they have excellent passive income ideas, are the ones who blog on everything without exception. It may appear to be bizarre since numerous people would imagine that these blogs would pull in more readers. In any case, readers need blogs to be about only a specific something. Sites with arbitrary themes aren't as prone to assemble a decent gathering of people as sites with a substantial core interest.

Genuinely fruitful bloggers will create something their readers need. These blogs additionally have very much focused on publicizing that will draw in that gathering of people. That is the reason that focused activity is so valuable. People who need to get all that they can out of blogging will assemble solid content and income streams that aren't anything but trying to disturb. The final product will be a genuinely fantastic dimension of money streaming in - effortlessly and with minimal extra work.

5 EASY PASSIVE INCOME IDEAS

Passive income is an objective or dream for some people, yet escapes some since they mostly don't realize where to start. We are not educated in school how to create passive income, how to land positions. As grown-ups a large portion of us winds up running in a similar rodent race as every other person, thinking about how we arrived and if there is a way out.

There is always a way out. Be that as it may, a large number of the choices appear to require a ton of money, a considerable measure of time, or illicit exercises. None of these are extremely speaking to the average individual. Here are five simple passive income ideas which don't require a great deal of either, and are lawful.

1. Article Writing

Article writing has turned out to be hugely famous in the most recent decade or something like that and can earn your money forthright and excessively. Sites like Hub Pages, Squidoo, and Associated Content pay you a repetitive sum dependent on what number of guests your page gets as well as what number of people click on the advertisements set on your page. The best part is that writing these articles or building these pages is without fun, and you can expound on nearly anything that intrigues you. If you can compose neatly and enthusiastically about your interests, you can start earning.

2. House/Property Income.

Earning house property income is tempting to numerous people, yet additionally somewhat frightening. When they think about the measure of money required to purchase a house, they close the book and turn away. This is disastrous because there are numerous alternatives to buy a house for no money down, regardless of whether you are not a first-time homebuyer. The principles of earning house property are quite basic: insofar as the house or property isn't utilized to lead your very own business, you may guarantee an income.

3. Affiliate Marketing

Affiliate marketing is like article writing in that it's a numbers amusement. The more people you acquaint your affiliate's item with, the higher your business rate. Regular ways of getting the word out are writing articles to submit to free registries, utilizing Craigslist promotions, and building small-scale sites for the item. Once more, no money is required to start marketing, and huge names like Amazon have an affiliate network you can join for nothing. As you earn, you can cycle a part of your benefits once more into your marketing, and get higher and higher returns. The sky's the limit here.

4. Gold Investing

Putting resources into gold is a smart thought in an economy. Gold happens to be one of only a handful couple of items which never lose much esteem if any whatsoever and it is all-inclusive. It is a genuine single market to learn, and you can be ready for action before long.

5. Websites

Nowadays anybody can construct a website. There are such vast numbers of apparatuses accessible that you don't have to know anything about coding, and each subject has a potential gathering of people. Start with an idea, discover a web host (some are under $6 every month), utilize their devices and support to get set up, compose or purchase content at a reduced rate, and publicize using long range interpersonal communication. The best sites are those who don't require constant upkeep. When assembled, you should need to spruce it up more than once per year. As you get guests, you get the consideration of publicists willing to pay you only for a spot on your site, and you don't need to offer anything! How much less demanding would it be able to get?

These five models are simply starter ideas for earning passive income rapidly and effectively. When you have even the littlest measure of revenue coming in, there are a huge number of different choices accessible for making much more. The way is altogether up to you.

PASSIVE INCOME IDEAS: THINK YOUR WAY TO THE BANK

How long do you get the chance to work and wish you could sit at your work area, do nothing and still get paid? Have you been attempting to figure out how to bring in money all alone? The idea of getting paid and not committing 40 hours per week to another person's motivation, ought to inspire enough to make them search for passive income ideas!

Passive income is money that comes in on a persistent premise after you put shortly of work to get this show on the road. As opposed to getting paid for the amount of time you put into whatever you're your setting is, you create a way to assemble something one time and it will keep on bringing money in. The objective behind this specific kind of income is to do as much work as you will do. What's more, gather on it for a significant lot of time.

Network Marketing

A standout amongst the most prominent and possibly the most seasoned of the majority of the passive income ideas would need to be network marketing. This is a business that is organized in levels. You turn into a merchant or subsidiary of a parent company that sells products or administrations. The most widely recognized of these companies, for the most part, sell restorative, consumables or fresh products. As you sell your stock, you enroll people to assemble a group. You at that point gather commissions from your colleagues' deals and your own. This specific idea works best when you have a decent estimated group.

Connections and Banners on Blogs

On the off chance that you are internet smart and have a blog page, you can utilize your blog page to create passive income. This is another way that can bring in a decent amount of money on a month to month premise. You can charge a little expense to companies and people who wish to publicize on your blog page by posting connections and flags that will direct people to their page. Web-based promoting is the manner by which companies achieve the majority. They need to publicize. On the off chance that you have space, why not utilize it to encourage them and yourself in the meantime.

Vending Machines

A surefire way to create passive income is putting resources into vending machines. You need to concede that each time you see one, you think about how much money the proprietor is gathering each time they refill. Also, every time one takes your money, you wish it was you! Vending machines are an incredible way to procure income that will be ceaseless. Your only concern will anchor contracts with areas and keeping the devices full.

Enrollment Sites

Having aptitude or something to that effect can be parlayed into passive income also. You can set up an enrollment site, which charges a month to month expense for access. For whatever length of time that you can keep a flood of activity going to your site, you will have money coming in consistently. This is for the most part ideal for people who have degrees in some zone and can offer administrations that merit is paying for.

Procuring money in any capacity other than a 9-5 doesn't need to be entangled. There is no motivation to go up against other employment and accomplish a more significant amount of what you do on the first. Getting paid dependent on your time has ended up being a drag and not extremely painful. A great many people usually are excessively worn out, making it impossible to appreciate their rewards for so much hard work.

With the number of passive income ideas to consider, there's no reason you shouldn't have the capacity to figure out how to bring in as much money as you need. No, you won't get wealthy in the first place. However, if you utilize your time astutely, you can make a decent amount of money. With the correct undertakings... you can transform that horrendous dependent on time pay into decent pay in no time.

Two Effective Passive Income Ideas

Numerous people are searching for passive income ideas to enable them to abandon financial imperatives. The way to economic freedom is one of the streets few have taken.

While it isn't hard to tread, it isn't for the fretful. What can be ensured however is that passive income is the key to financial freedom? What's more, on the off chance that it is the thing that you are searching for, you have gone to the correct page.

On the off chance that you are sick of working for huge hours out of every day and still not have enough to put something aside for retirement, the arrangement is appropriate here.

If you are knee-somewhere down paying off debtors with not a single clear answer for being seen, you need not go anyplace else for the appropriate responses.

If you are reluctant to begin a family for dread you probably won't have enough to pass by, now's the time to change that.

If you think you are overworked yet at the same time don't have enough, you need to drop your work and search for passive income ideas.

No, this isn't a lie. You won't be approached to pay anything for this data. It is conceivable to free yourself from the abundance stuff cause by your funds.

Try not to put stock in the prattle that you never again need to work when you as of now have passive income. Indeed, passive income requires genuine work.

There is no quick forward to getting to that street. Give these passive income ideas a chance to take you there.

Microstock

Microstock is the selling of illustrations over the web. You should transfer them to specific sites and let the sections deal with the rest.

What these sites will do is sell the images and you at that point acquire from each deal they make. The more pictures you have that moves toward becoming hits in the market, the more income you get.

This is one way of having something that can influence you to win for a lifetime.

The main thing you need for this income idea is the aptitude of making images and recordings. When you have supplied enough photos, you can quit making more pictures and still procure more.

Internet Marketing

While Microstock requires specific aptitudes, internet marketing does not need such. On the off chance that you don't have realistic aptitudes, this can be the alternative for you.

You can work from home and procure more than microstock does.

Subsidiary marketing is the most effortless way to enable you to get your objectives. You should advance items through a specific website and acquire a commission each time somebody buys through that site.

It, for the most part, implies that you need to create a specialty, compose profitable substance, and create movement. This is with the end goal to advance the items you publicized. It's that simple, yet it has given various people relentless income throughout the years.

These passive income ideas have turned out to be viable and workable. Pick which is feasible for you and begin from that point. Keep in mind this can be your way to financial freedom so pick carefully.

HOW TO GET PASSIVE INCOME IDEAS FROM THE INTERNET MARKETING FORUMS: A BRAINSTORMING GUIDE!

There are many internet marketing forums online that let the internet advertisers talk about and share their ideas and get their appropriate JV accomplices. In the meantime, these marketplaces are considered as great assets for the new advertisers who need to learn and venture into the universe of internet marketing. In case you're a beginner and need a rule, you certainly need to enlist yourself on a portion of these places and start learning things today! You will explore a large number of ideas and methods being shared on these forums every day; in case you're an action taker, you can start making money in no time. In any case, here you will find how you can learn and explore passive income ideas from these internet marketing forums.

Getting Passive Income Ideas From The Internet Marketing Forums: How And Where To Start!

These internet marketing forums are generally allowed to enroll; this implies you don't need to contribute anything to start learning the stuff. The best thing is you don't should be experienced to begin learning from these places. The arbitrators and individuals are extremely useful, and they are always quick to give others a chance to learn and explore the potential methods. Be that as it may, if you don't realize where and how to start, it might take more time to start making money. In this way, we should find how to make it quicker and powerful:

#1 Joining the most well-known marketplaces

There are truly a large number of places that merit joining; however, it's an awful idea to pursue such huge amounts of places. Better you waitlist the most famous ones and enter the main five among them. This will guarantee you get the appropriate presentation to the essential stuff and besides, some propelled material. The learning procedure will be better on the off chance that you have a lot of assets to learn from.

#2 Remaining dynamic and read the posts from the accomplished individuals

When you have joined a couple of the best forums committed to internet marketing, it's time to center around learning things without any preparation. Regardless of whether you have fundamental ideas about two or three jobs, you ought to consider modifying the nuts and bolts and make your base more grounded. You ought to be dynamic on these forums, partake in dialogs and ask the senior individuals to learn all the more successfully.

#3 Downloads, complimentary gifts and make money areas

There are a few areas on pretty much every internet marketing forum. When you have gone along with, you need to explore the forums and discover some specific places to get devices, aides, methods and everything else to start making money. First, you have to study downloads and complimentary gifts segment. Here you will discover loads of apparatuses that are basics to start. Additionally, consider visiting the make money area to get the methods that work. Discover what plans are being prevalent and pursue a reasonable one among them.

#4 You ought to maintain a strategic distance from two or three stuff!

As an amateur, you must be cautious about two or three things on these marketplaces. You have to maintain a strategic distance from several kinds of stuff. You to play with alert while downloading anything; additionally, you ought to be cautious about purchasing anything too. Consider perusing the remarks and criticisms before you arrange something on the marketplaces.

Passive Income Ideas: Ways to Get the Cash Rolling In

Is it accurate to say that you are keen on earning money without executing yourself working for it? Does the idea of having money coming in on a regular basis get you energized? Is it true that you are burnt out on being paid dependent on how long of work you've put in? Assuming this is the case, you ought to consider becoming required with something that will earn your passive income.

Passive income is income that keeps on coming in over the long run after you have completed an insignificant measure of work. Insignificant implies that the most work you will do will be at the start of your endeavor. When you are set up, there is little support work that should be finished. As a rule, week by week support is sufficient to keep the money streaming. There are numerous passive income ideas to contemplate.

Vending Machines

Extraordinary compared to other passive income ideas is to put resources into a vending machine business. Although this is one of the more exorbitant ideas, there is almost no work required on your part. Your fundamental concern will discover areas to place your vending machines and keeping them loaded. When the tools are in the area, you kick back and hold up to gather.

Composing eBooks

Not every person has seed money to put into a business opportunity. There are passive income ideas dependent on attractive abilities, for example, composing. Composing an eBook is a conventional method to earn money on a regular basis. The way to this idea is to pick a point that is popular and to advance it appropriately. Each time the eBook is bought, you will earn. When this is the heading that you go, it is ideal to have more than one eBook available. The stream towards eBooks can be little, to augment your income likely outcomes, various eBooks on various points is suggested.

Stock Dividends

One more of the incredible passive income ideas to mull over is to make budgetary speculations. Becoming an investor in an organization that pays profits to their speculators is a conventional method to guarantee that you will have money coming in on a constant basis. Most organizations pay benefits quarterly. What number of offers you hold, decides how much your interest will pay out.

There are a lot of chances to earn advantageous income that streams on a constant basis. To show them all would take until the end of time. The objective is to discover something that will pay you the most, with little work or exertion on your part. It would likewise be incautious to contribute more than what you would find consequently in a short measure of time.

Passive income ideas can be different. Some will cost you or nothing; while others may require a generous measure of seed money. How much physical work you have put in, is likewise founded on what you do. Which idea works best for you, is entirely up to your attentiveness. Remember that you are hoping to create an income that you will see week after week, after a seemingly endless amount of time or a seemingly infinite amount of time.

HOW TO MAKE MONEY THROUGH DROP SHIPPING?

Numerous destinations and books guarantee your methods for making several dollars every day through at home organizations. Vast numbers of these destinations and books are composed by tricksters who deceive you into giving them a considerable measure of cash for next to no consequences. This isn't one of those. This section records various genuine ways that a stay at home business visionary or little businessperson or lady can make a benefit through outsourcing. This isn't a trick since I'm not saying that you will gain a great deal of cash rapidly; it will in all likelihood set aside you an extended opportunity to win a considerable measure of money through outsourcing alone. In any case, if you are a stay at home parent or a low-pay worker who needs to enhance their profit through internet exchange, then you should peruse this section and discover how to utilize outsourcing further bolstering your advantage.

Outsourcing is a real business practice that has been utilized and manhandled for a long time. Fundamentally; when a retailer offers and a thing that they don't physically have in their store, they are outsourcing. A little specialty business, for example, a bicycle shop may have a couple of models of a bicycle in store, and they take orders from the client when offering the products. The retailer will then contact the producer or distributor and inspire them to send the merchandise straightforwardly to the clients. As a rule, the producer or distributor will name the crate with the retailer's location, so the client conceives that it was the bicycle shop that sent the merchandise and not the distributor or maker.

You can utilize this procedure further bolstering your advantage if you wish to profit from home. Numerous wholesalers and producers have their sites online where you can check their stock and check whether anything hops out at you. You would then be able to set up an eBay account or your site through which to offer these things. Since the distributor or producer will outsource, you will never have any contact with the real stock hence killing the requirement for you to have a customer facing facade.

If this sounds like a smart thought, here are a couple of things to consider:

In many nations, wholesalers will pitch to authentic organizations so you may need to enroll yourself or your site as an independent venture. This implies you should be recorded for expense purposes.

Ensure you comprehend the profits approach from the distributor. On the off chance that a client is sent flawed great they will reach you, so you need to realize what you can do to help them.

The benefit will originate from the distinction in cost between what you purchase the things for and what you offer them for, yet you will likewise get rehash clients if you provide quality things. Attempt to discover the harmony between a shoddy distributer and one that has excellent quality stock.

Monitoring Your Suppliers

One approach to elevate your things is to request that your provider's consent do the pressing of your products since these will empower you to embed flyers and cash off vouchers in the bundling. Separation ought to likewise not be an obstruction for you to screen how well your removed providers are serving your clients. Top eBay Power sellers have clear privileged insights that you have to fuse inside you to resemble them - comprehend what's hot in the business, make utilization of outsourcing to caution as much as possible, and get your work done by inquiring about on the items that are offering like hotcakes in the internet offering industry.

What is outsourcing at that point? It is something that is generally drilled now by a considerable measure of retailers since it is an issue free approach to send mass requests straightforwardly from the wholesalers to the buyers without going through the retailer. Instead of application a large main part of items to stock inside the house, retailers influence utilization of drop shippers with the goal that they too don't need to put an excessive number of supplies of one item in their homes. You can gain your benefit through the value that you charge. What you have to do is settle on a thing to offer, make a closeout posting for it, and provide it there. When the closeout completes, you get paid by the victor. You procure your benefit through the distinction between your purchasing cost and offering cost. A pleasant thing about outsourcing is that you can do your business anyplace and all over the place, as long as you have a web association.

Another beneficial thing about outsourcing is that you can maintain the business amid your spare time. There will be extra expenses, and you most likely won't get the chance to keep even 50% of the retail cost, in addition to you need to pay for some eBay charges. Additionally, since the outsourcing will send your items for you, you have to send them your marks with the goal that they can fuse them in your questions.

Understanding the Dropshipping Business

Happens in outsourcing that they offer things at discount costs, and afterward convey those things straightforwardly to the location of your buyer. The provider deals with all the business. This will give you more opportunity to center around your business methodologies, accordingly drawing in more clients to purchase your things.

CHAPTER TWO

HOW TO MAKE MONEY ON EBAY WITH DROPSHIPPING?

Bringing home, the bacon on eBay is numerous individuals' fantasy. Offering on eBay and making a significant benefit isn't as simple as it used to be. Be that as it may, it is as yet conceivable to bring home the bacon online as long as you discover right way. Today, an ever-increasing number of individuals are offering items on eBay with outsourcing, does outsourcing honestly work? Why a few people who are delivering on eBay progressed toward becoming force vendors and the others fizzled? For what reason are those power merchants truly utilizing outsourcing? The appropriate response is yes and no!

In the first place, we need to comprehend what outsourcing is. Outsourcing is that retailer does not keep merchandise in stock. Instead, they exchange client requests and shipment data straightforwardly to wholesalers, who at that point dispatch the products straight to the client. Consequently, you don't need to hold stock and handle the shipment.

Although numerous people who offer online joined the drop shipping organization, not every person utilizes dropshipping, at any rate, not eBay power sellers. The more significant part of them utilize drop shippers as wholesale suppliers, yet I can let you know without a doubt that they don't utilize drop shipping, perhaps at starting they did. We should confront reality: resale (buying and re-selling for a profit) is tied in with buying power, and with dropshipping, you have none! Since you are regularly buying only one item, you have no buying power. Genuine wholesale valuing is about the amount. Remembering: when you utilize drop shipping, you will pay a marginally higher wholesale price for a single item to be conveyed to your customer. Since you spend a somewhat higher rate, it is slightly harder to contend in your product advertise.

Even though you pay a somewhat higher wholesale price, you don't need to purchase a group of products in beef in advance, and expectation that you offer them. Accordingly, the genuine favorable position of utilizing a wholesale drop shipping supplier is at the beginning requiring little to no effort, and TESTING diverse products without a lot of costs. Before you begin to offer on eBay, you need to comprehend what product purchasers need. You would prefer not to dropship staggeringly popular items since you are never going to make money with them. In any case, on the off chance that you do inquire about you can observe items to be focused with and make money.

Where would you be able to discover what purchasers need? In eBay seller's My eBay page, you can discover the connection: Want It Now! Through that page, you can discover what purchasers need, and after that seek dropship suppliers.

When you discover a product from a wholesale dropship supplier that functions admirably, the time has come to begin buying that product in mass, and ship them yourself. Most eBay power sellers are selling products with this strategy. You can show signs of improvement price parts from the supplier that way, and your retail price descends. This enables you to contend in the market all the more effective.

If you need to have a business that offers on eBay or Amazon, you need to understand that dropshipping is anything but a permanent arrangement. Utilizing a wholesale dropship supplier for beginning at a low price and for product testing, it is a stage en route to requesting and stocking products in mass.

Step by step instructions to Make Money Online With Blogging Or Dropshipping

Blogging is a fun way to make money. One thing to remember is you need to love to compose, and you must have an enthusiasm to write. The way to be fruitful at blogging is to discover your specialty; your energy may be, it's what you will expound on. You can explain anything regarding the matter, or present all in all subject. Keep in mind do your examination on it before regardless of whether you think you know everything. Record inquiries to look into, because it will help you later on. One model would be, what would people like to hear most about a subject? You are there to move people, not merely make a jettison or two of them.

There are various ways to make money with your blog. Even though, it shouldn't be only for the money. One way to make money is through affiliate marketing. Affiliate marketing is the place a business pays you a commission to bring them, customers. You would generally put standards or connections onto your blog. A well-known way to make money is through Pay-per-click promoting. Rather than getting a commission, you would get money each time someone taps on the pennant or connection. A lot of businesses have affiliate or accomplice on the base of the organization's page. You need to join. You can likewise attempt ClickBank. The extraordinary news is most organizations given you a chance to pick how to get paid. Most have PayPal, so you don't need to stress over your financial records.

Drop shipping is another extraordinary way to make money. Shockingly, it's additionally misjudged. A lot of people go into it supposing they will make a slaughtering selling on eBay. The Truth about drop shipping is, all drop shippers are not made the equivalent. Some charge excessively for their products, in addition to a mess of different expenses and costs. Avoid those sort! There are drop shippers that will charge a little fee, and there are others that are free. You shouldn't pay a lot of money to join these sorts of businesses. You need to make a profit, also, to have the capacity to rival different sellers.

There are organizations out there that have lists of drop shippers, yet more often than not you should pay for the lists. There are some free ones, however from what I have seen they are not by any stretch of the imagination a la mode. A portion of the beneficial things about buying the lists are, you don't need to make a trip to public expos, and you won't need to sit on the web for a considerable length of time hunting down great drop shippers. A useful bit of advice, there are a lot of tricks going on, another valid justification to run with a paid list. Simply make beyond any doubt you're not paying excessively. There shouldn't be the month to month charges, and it shouldn't be anything with a huge sticker price. Run with the more significant names in the business. Salehoo or World Wide Brands are a decent place to begin. Keep in mind, you're not getting an entire genuine deal from a portion of the drop shippers on the list, however, take a gander at it along these lines, you're not going to have a lot of overhead either. It indeed works itself out.

Keep in mind, do your examination before beginning your endeavor. Trust me; it will be justified, despite all the trouble over the long haul. Make beyond any doubt you are cheerful first. Regardless of whether you pick blogging or dropshipping, If you do it right, odds are you will be a win. Good fortunes and appreciate!

MAKE MONEY THROUGH WHOLESALE DROP SHIPPING - THE NEW E-BUSINESS FOR THE ELECTRONIC WORLD

Not merely your customary website.

Have you known about Wholesale Drop Shipping? It is the point at which you exchange items on the web, and afterward, you put the orders to the dropship provider who consequently convey the theme to your customer.

Its more specialized meaning is a production network the board method in which the retailer does not keep merchandise in stock, but instead exchanges customer orders and shipment points of interest to either the producer or a distributor, who at that point ships the merchandise specifically to the customer.

Drop shipping is the place the retailer does not keep any stock in stock and which is usually utilized via mail order, list and internet businesses to offer the customer a wide assortment of items without making speculation for their inventory. Endeavor to visit Salehoo website, it has an incredible asset for the two learners and experienced drop shippers, since they have a wide rundown of suppliers and organizations that offer wholesaling and drop shipping.

The parcel of people currently wins through the online business like drop shipping. It is presently your opportunity to set up your business in the solace of your own home. By basically having a PC and internet association you can start your very own drop shipping business. You don't need to be a business virtuoso; extraordinary abilities are not required in this industry. All you need is only essential learning in PC and utilization of the internet.

In what capacity will you win cash through this drop shipping?

You will fill in as a center individual/go between the drop ship provider and your customer. You are the one answerable in getting orders from the customer, and the dropship provider will be the one to convey the product to the customer. You will win by the contrast between your offering price and the price you need to pay the drop ship provider. In drop shipping, you have the ton to put resources into types of gear or stock a pack of inventory. You are into an all retail businesses. You make the profit on the distinction between the discount and your retail price.

In this strategy we can decrease if not to dispose of duplication of exertion alongside related costs as just a single part in the chain (distributor) needs to 'pick, pack and ship' the product which results to the decrease of costs in the store network. It certainly decreases add up to inventory the board and shipping costs which can be passed on to the customer. Likewise, backorders can be limited by coordinating your shopping basket with your supplier's inventory accessibility framework/programming. That will help keep away from both backorders and order scratch-offs because on the absence of inventory — all as to lessen cost and increment profit.

Salehoo Wholesale Drop shippers is always refreshing their database and can provide universal shipping at low or no base order amounts. There is likewise A three-level audit arrangement of Salehoo licensed drop shippers are done to guarantee nature of products and administrations.

Dropshipping and E-commerce - How to Make Money When Times Are Tough

If you resemble the lion's share of Americans, you are feeling the squeeze on your wallet this Christmas season. Joblessness is soaring, and we are on the whole discovering it progressively hard to win a sustainable living. Be that as it may, there is promise for those of us who need some additional money this season, and that trust is through online dropshipping!

Dropshipping permits standard internet clients like

you and me to rapidly and effortlessly showcase products online without the issues of buying inventory, bundling or shipping. Just enroll with an online drop shipping administration, advertise their products online at your price, and keep the distinction after the deal! This administration is made conceivable because dropshipping organizations secretly ship their products straightforwardly to your customers. To the extent your customer knows, he is managing solely with you and your online business.

eBay and Amazon.com are excellent choices for those new to drop shipping online. With negligible costs, new drop shippers can try things out of online web based business and endeavor to exchange appeal products to a broad customer gathering of people. Although eBay may charge an ostensible posting expense to offer your product, Amazon.com will, for the most part, gather a little rate when your product provides. Or on the other hand, even better, showcase an assortment of products from your drop shipping supplier all alone web-based business website and rapidly fabricate a devoted customer base.

I initially dug into the universe of dropshipping to help pay charges as a college understudy. The procedure was accessible to the point that I before long started offering everything from kitchen container to dishwashers. If an understudy can exchange $500+ dishwashers online with positively no learning about the product, at that point, you can as well!

The initial step to the beginning in the realm of drop shipping is to locate the correct supplier. Be additional watchful in picking your supplier because not evident product wholesalers control all drop shipping websites. One of the greatest threats in the dropshipping business is finding a supplier who is extremely an agent; on the off chance that you don't locate a genuine supplier, the product evaluating will be higher, and your profits will be lower! As opposed to searching for suppliers utilizing a search engine, I suggest that you agree to accept a database to guarantee that you approach the best products at the most reasonable prices!

When you have discovered your suppliers, the rest is simple! Just select the products that you wish to exchange, post those products in an online closeout or all alone web-based business website at a slight markup price, and trust that customers will buy your products. At the point when your business starts coming in, forward the order data to your, and they will deal with the rest!

Step by step instructions to Make Money Online Through Reselling and Dropshipping

Try not to have the funding to start your own online business? We have the answer for you. Did you realize that you can at present do your own online business without having a startup spending plan? You should locate the correct supplier for exchanging and get into the new plan of dropshipping. Trading has been a long-term alternative for a ton of starting businessmen and ladies in the online world. There is a considerable measure of organizations online that offer discount and retail products that you can set up as preordered merchandise for your purchasers.

To start the way toward acquiring from these two strategies, you should initially locate the correct site page to execute your business. However much as could reasonably be expected, make the structure of your website fascinating to pick up a considerable measure of watchers and shopper consideration. When you have set up your site, you would now be able to start searching for your supplier. If you choose to offer garments, for example, you can visit any search engine and search for the absolute most dependable garments suppliers online. When you have gotten all the data that you need, you can start exchanging the items on your website. You can include your coveted sum best of the first prices to show signs of improvement profit.

By pre-ordering, your customers will provide you with their installment early and will trust that their products will land at their doorstep. You can exploit the dropshipping plan, which considers your supplier responsible for pressing your products and shipping them straightforwardly to your customers. The drop shipper will compose your name as the sender of the bundle to appear as though the product came straight from you like the dealer. Through this procedure, you need not to provide your own money to make your business fruitful.

HOW TO FIND PRODUCTS TO DROP SHIP AND SUCCESSFULLY MAKE MONEY

With such a significant number of people needing to make money using drop shipping I figured it would be an incredible time to give a straightforward well-ordered manual for finding a worthwhile product to drop dispatch. Numerous people fail to make money from drop shipping, and they frequently put this down to the way that it is an over advertised business adventure that isn't as beneficial as it has been developed to be. In truth anyway, the reason people fail is that they just haven't discovered a good enough market, more often than not because of an absence of research.

Indeed, before you even discover an organization that dropships you should find out what market you need to offer in and sees whether it is a market you can prevail in.

You are undeniably liable to succeed on the off chance that you can discover what is ordinarily known as a niche market as the opposition will be far less. Essentially a niche market is a section of greater demand. For instance, a broad market would be child products so a niche market would be something, for example, infant baby buggies, or if there is still a lot of rivalries, you could go even little and pick a specific brand of carriages to offer. Just put the less competition you have, the more prominent your shot of progress.

You can get general thoughts in a few places. One could be your very own diversions and intrigue. For example, if you are into cultivating take a gander at the items, you use to share in this leisure activity and think about them as conceivable markets. Somewhere else to discover thoughts is by essentially checking out the house and thinking about whether it is something you would think about purchasing online, on the off chance that you would you can wager others would as well.

There are a few places you can get a good thought of whether a market has buyers or not. Two right places to start are eBay heartbeat and glancing through Amazons classes and after that its smash hits inside these classifications.

At long last, once you have a market as a top priority go to eBay itself and look for your market. Presently you have the outcomes in front of you it is conceivable to see whether people are purchasing these items or not by tapping on cutting-edge inquiry and ticking the complete listings box at that point look. The outcomes will now indicate late items that have been placed up in this market, and whether they sold or not unfortunately if details are unsold more frequently than sold, I would advise you to investigate another market.

Making these strides should expand the odds of you making an ethical dimension of benefit from your dropshipping adventure as you should now have a completely looked into the list of products to dropship. All that you require now is to discover a drop shipper that offers the products you are hoping to provide yourself with.

Dropshipping - A Simple Way to Make Money Online with Retail Goods

If you have attempted your hand at offering stock previously, you realize that it is so essential to keep items in stock and look after stock. That is the customary way of providing retail. Be that as it may, because of the Internet, it is not anymore a prerequisite for you to keep a supply of what you suggest. You should know merely to set up a website and join a dropshipping network. Drop shipping is undoubtedly one of the simplest ways to make money online by offering retail goods.

How does drop shipping work? In simple terms, dropshipping is a way of offering goods online without these goods going through your hands. You go about as an agent between your buyer and your supplier without taking care of the goods physically yourself. Taking care of the stock and the shipment of the product itself is finished by the supplier.

When you choose to participate in drop shipping, the principal thing you have to do is to join a dropshipping network. There are numerous such networks online. You should pay for their enrollment, yet consequently, you gain admittance to different apparatuses to enable you to offer your products and degree your rivals, and to a restrictive list of suppliers. From this list, you pick the products you need to have some expertise in and offer it on your website - either an eBay page, a pre-planned site given by your network, or a webpage that you thought of individually.

The products made accessible by suppliers to the network come at discount prices, so it is dependent upon you to make your markup and decide your net revenue. You get the chance to list your prices for these products on your site. At whatever point somebody places a request for a product on your site, your activity is to make beyond any doubt that the application is like this set with the supplier. The supplier forms the buy and ships it to the buyer without you regularly observing it. The buyer pays at the product at the cost you listed, you pay the supplier the product's discount price, and you get the chance to keep the distinction. The whole methodology is pure and simple; you require an excellent website to feature your products.

If you need to make money online through online retailing, dropshipping is unquestionably one thing that you should attempt. This section is only a diagram of how dropshipping functions, and you should try to find out as much about it as you can. It is a pure and straightforward process that you can benefit from.

MAKING MONEY ONLINE WITH DROPSHIPPING EXPLAINED

Making money online through drop-shipping is entirely pure on the off chance that you recognize what to do and how to do it. Extraordinary compared to other ways to start making money on the Internet is by creating a web-based business webpage that will purchase and offer different discount and closeout stock. Making money online through drop-shipping is a superb open door for some people. In any case, this is the reality that a few people fail to make money online while others make a fortune with this chance.

What Is Ecommerce?

Web-based business or Electronic Commerce (EC) is the way toward leading business exchanges in a virtual financial condition. An online store is turning into a remunerating adventure. It is proceeding to confront difficulties all through the passing years. It has stroked the current deals and marketing methods.

E-commerce is perfect for niche products. E-commerce is digging in for the long haul and some its officially second nature with regards to shopping. Others may require some additionally persuading that their money and individual subtle elements will stay safe should they ever choose to purchase something online. E-commerce is the most recent pattern in the flourishing online business field. As its name infers, e-commerce is about electronic commerce, and it gives business people an intuitive online stage to do business.

Dropshipping Explained

Drop shipping is a simple course of action that empowers you to offer superb products at low discount prices while never putting away, handle or ship stock. You can offer products on your website, blog, or through a bartering website, for example, eBay or Amazon. Drop Shippers are Wholesale Suppliers who send products specifically to your Customer's entryway, from the stockroom. You don't pay in advance to stock products. Drop shipping is extremely powerful, and numerous dealers are doing.

Drop shipping is a business that had been restricted to huge mail arrange organizations. In any case, with the approach of the web, drop-shipping ended up accessible to independent venture. Drop-shipping is presently settled as a gainful online business shape; notwithstanding, finding reliable wholesalers and drop shippers remains an outstanding issue for the vast majority of the start-ups. Dropship business can't bloom without some genuine discount supplier or wholesaler at its back.

HOW TO MAKE MONEY AFFILIATE MARKETING AS A NEWBIE?

Numerous people have seen advertisements, or websites elevating how to make money affiliate marketing. The real truth is you can make money affiliate marketing on the off chance that you realize how to target people later in the purchasing cycle. Offering people something isn't the appropriate response. Nobody likes utilized vehicle salespeople, and nobody likes pushy utilized vehicle salesperson.

With the end goal to make money affiliate marketing you need to take in a few skills like:

- Niche inquire about
- What are great purchasing keywords
- What to offer
- How to compose compelling duplicate and reviews?
- How to fabricate a point of arrival?
- How to set up a website and pick in for email marketing

I realize you suppose who knows all that, and the appropriate response is nobody.

Much the same as an occupation skill, you need to figure out how to make money affiliate marketing by utilizing compelling methods that draw people through a pipe and transform them into purchasers.

At the point when people are beginning they get enveloped with adapting each skill to make money affiliate marketing. Stop, this is the wrong methodology, and you need to pick a bearing and make a move from the begin. Make a timetable to pursue.

In the first place, you will need a target audience, and a set of firmly centered niche keywords and something to offer them. This step should take the more significant part of your time and realize precisely what your audience needs and needs. At that point offer it to them.

Next, you need the movement to your review site and a way to persuade your target audience you have the leading solution for their needs. Offer a reward if they buy, offer support and help, something that makes you remain over the rest.

Keep in mind, and you need a way to lead people from your review site or blog to make a buy. With such a significant number of people utilizing web-based life properties you can find gatherings of people and join the discussion. On the off chance that you can assist them with an issue, they will tail you.

In conclusion, to figure out how to make money affiliate marketing pick a course, paid or free (incorporates SEO) and stay with it. Archive each step of your adventure, track joins, sites, where people originated from, as these are all ways to figure out how to make money affiliate marketing quick.

Instructions to Make Money - Affiliate Marketing Without A Website

Here comes the genuine transformation, profiting on the Internet without really having a website and if somebody at any point composed a book on this they should name it "how to make money - affiliate marketing without a website."

There are a large number of ways you can win money. However, this little method requires nothing from you, and it's smooth to the point that it doesn't need for you to have your website. Affiliate business keeps running on the guideline of acquainting an obscure individual with a specific brand and if that individual purchases something from that brand you are given a decent amount for doing your part in familiarizing that individual with that brand.

Sounds confounding? We should make it simple, if 'An' experiences passionate feelings for 'X' A discussion about 'X' to 'C' and the 'C' needs to give 'X' a shot and the procedure duplicates. FYI 'X' is not a female.

There are different methods of doing it, sending an email with the brand affiliate connect to your companions or to gatherings of people you know. On the off chance that they click on the connection and purchase something from that brand, you get the opportunity to keep a little offer. Now and again a few products accompany an affiliate program, and if you have utilized that specific product and you have delighted in it, you could prescribe it to people enlightening them regarding the product on the internet and guide them to the website.

Likewise, we can post recordings on video-sharing websites and afterward direct people to the site helping the brand with marketing essentially. The more people visit, the better you would procure.

All you are doing is utilizing a product and afterward getting it out to the group, in a few words you can call it web-based marketing. To make money, affiliate marketing without a website is an unbelievable thought since it requires the slightest skill and the minimum of endeavors.

Instructions to Make Money - Affiliate Marketing - Step by Step Method to Making Money Online

Such a significant number of people in this present economy need to realize how to make money affiliate marketing. The possibility of lying in bed around evening time recognizing that money is being deposited into your record with negligible exertion is enticing to the point that numerous new internet marketers get sucked into scam after scam. Lamentably, there are various scammers in the field of internet marketing who gather $27 here and $97 there offering minimal other than reiterated free material that any marketer would have the capacity to access individually. The reality of how to make money affiliate marketing is relatively simple when you pursue the steps plot underneath:

- **Find a niche:** How would you find a niche? Utilize the Google keyword apparatus to reveal the number of quests being done every month. This will give you a thought about what amount of searches are done every month and how gainful your battle might be.

- **Find out your opposition:** Look at Google to perceive what number of contending websites there are for your keyword. Anything over around 20,000 might be challenging to rival utilizing free marketing methods.

• When you have picked your niche, start composing articles for the free article indexes and additionally making Squidoo focal points about your subject. Be mindful of utilizing your keyword expression inside your items to amplify website improvement.

• Consider digging into PPC (Pay Per Click) marketing efforts. When you check that you have a money-making affiliate marketing program, you should need to consider attempting a littler scale Pay Per Click crusade. This is regularly the most straightforward and quickest way to make real money in affiliate marketing. Be cautious that you have practical training before you endeavor PPC, in any case, since you can without much of a stretch LOSE money if you don't comprehend what you are doing!

• You can make money affiliate marketing if you recognize what you are doing and have the correct training and support you need! Pursue an arrangement, don't get off track and remain concentrated on your real objectives.

- Having SUPPORT is a critical component of turning into a TOP internet marketer. Imagine a scenario where there was where you could talk day by day to TOP affiliate marketers, get two months of REAL training and a FREE website developer, in addition to TONS more. Look at this if you are SERIOUS about this business.

CHAPTER THREE

FIND OUT HOW TO MAKE MONEY AFFILIATE MARKETING

For any individual who needs to start an online business from home, you most likely realize that the measure of data online can be overpowering. You may have known about system marketing, sometimes alluded to as MLM, or affiliate marketing yet you may not see the contrast between the two. If you do know the distinction, you may think that its difficult to begin. You are most likely considering how you can do money with affiliate marketing or MLM marketing.

There are a great many resources accessible online, yet you must be watchful. When you start visiting websites, you will start getting offers for different work from home business openings. The vast majority of these offers will likely be from authentic businesses; a couple will be tricks; however whichever way you would prefer not to spend any money now for locally established business openings. This is where most 'novices' make botches. A great many people do it in reverse. You wouldn't go out to apply for an unusual state office work before you set off for college, okay? That is the thing that a lot of people online do. They attempt to start offering affiliate products before they know anything about how to market online.

You need to instruct yourself in how to market online. This instruction can come in numerous structures, software, digital books, bulletins, e-courses, forums, and so forth. There are multiple ways to instruct yourself and show you how to make money affiliate marketing. A portion of these resources will be free and some you should pay for. If you have some extra money to contribute this is the place to start. Try not to squander your time or money on the most recent and greatest 'make money presently' program. Regardless of how enticing or how great the program is, and there are some extremely great programs around, on the off chance that you don't realize how to market it and direct people to your website (not to mention figure out how, it's simple, to set up a website) you won't figure out how to make money affiliate marketing.

So you need to get the instruction you need to make money affiliate marketing, now where do you go? The initial step is to complete a look for forums. Utilize look terms like internet marketing forums, online marketing forums, and so on. Discover a few forums and join. At that point invest a little energy there as frequently as possible. Alert: you must be extremely watchful of two potential traps with panels. One, they can be a shelter for 'complainers.' A few people get a kick out of the chance to gripe, and on the off chance that you give careful consideration to the grumblers it will make it troublesome for you to keep an inspirational mentality.

What's more, two, you can squander a lot of time. Your time in a forum can go up against its very own actual existence. Try not to dawdle. Get in, get out.

All in all, when you're at the forum, what explicitly would you say you are searching for? By what means can a conference enable you to discover how to make money affiliate marketing? Attempt to focus on the territories that examine new products, suggested products. You need to find the devices that will give you the training you need. Numerous people who take an interest in the forums are incredibly proficient and will more than happy to assist the 'amateur' you should inquire. You would be astonished at the excellent, free training you can get on a forum.

INSTRUCTIONS TO MAKE MONEY WITH AFFILIATE MARKETING

We as a whole realize that the economy is harried. Employments are rare as is money when gas costs and the cost of everything else is high as can be people are feeling the squeeze like never before. Numerous people are endeavoring to get extra money. The web can be a great way to make some extra cash, possibly quit your regular employment sooner or later. In any case, what is the ideal way online to make money? Should it indeed be possible? How might you make money with affiliate marketing?

For those of you knew to the term, affiliate marketing alludes to offering other peoples' products, usually electronic products, for example, digital books, sounds, and software. For everything sold, you will get a commission. It is free to join to end up an affiliate. You will get a free repeated website where your bonuses will be followed consequently. That is affiliate marketing more or less.

With affiliate marketing similarly as with a business, you need to get clients to your website to make any money. Clients online can come through different online marketing techniques. The ideal way to make money affiliate marketing is to figure out how to market successfully online. Learning online marketing systems isn't too hard, yet you should take some time and figure out how. Don't merely toss your money at compensation for every snap battle and seek after the best. That is a decent way to lose your shirt.

So where do you go to locate the instructive apparatuses you need to make money affiliate marketing?

The primary spot to start is to ask anyone you may realize who is an online marketer on the off chance that you don't understand anybody like that the following best thing is an endeavor to discover forums that are devoted to how to make money affiliate marketing. A large number of these forums are frequented by different affiliates, a large number of them the 'super affiliates,' top workers in affiliate marketing. A large portion of these marketers will readily pass on essential data; you should inquire.

Try not to be hesitant to 'pick their minds.' Make your inquiries. This is a standout amongst other ways to increase significant data on the most proficient method to make money affiliate marketing.

There are likewise several affiliate marketing software programs that can furnish you with exceedingly valuable resources. Once more, the forums are a decent place to start. Discover what other people are utilizing and prescribing.

You can likewise go to Clickbank.com or CommissionJunction.com and look at the affiliate marketing software. Locate the hot vendors with a low discount rate, and you are likely going to get an exceptionally supportive device.

The primary concern is: money is tight, don't squander it. Put in some money on affiliate marketing software, teach yourself on web marketing strategies. Set aside the opportunity to learn before you shop online, and you will spare yourself many migraines and money. You can make money affiliate marketing yet you need to figure out how first!

The most effective method to Make Money Affiliate Marketing

A lot of people attempt to get associated with affiliate marketing yet they rapidly surrender since they don't realize where to start. There is such a significant amount of data out there saying this and saying that, that it sometimes gets exceptionally disappointing and befuddling. With this section, I am going to rapidly make you through the strides you need to take to start making money affiliate marketing.

The first thing you need to do is join with an affiliate

arrange. There is a massive amount of them out there. However, I prescribe you start with ClickBank. When you have joined experience the marketplace and discovered a product, you might want to promote. A couple of things to search for when picking a product is one the gravity and two check whether the merchant gives you any materials to enable you to promote the product.

On ClickBank, the gravity of the product indicates what number of people have made a deal inside the most recent two months. A high gravity tells you that the product does deal which is something worth being thankful for. You likewise need to look at the merchant's affiliate page to perceive what they need to assist their affiliates. A few merchants will give books, official statements, watchwords and significantly more.

At the point when a merchant furnishes you with materials, it makes it a lot less demanding for you to get out there and start profiting. When you need to do all the examination yourself to concoct content, it can back things off significantly. When you have picked the product, you need to promote set up a straightforward blog and start advancing. The more substance you have out there, the more money you will make.

HOW TO MAKE MONEY WITH AFFILIATE MARKETING - 3 EASY STEPS

Turning into an affiliate marketer is one of the best ways to start profiting online. You can do it from the solaces of your own home, or on the off chance that you don't have a PC you can go to a nearby library or anyplace else that has open web get to. It is incredibly straightforward and here are the means to begin.

Promote 1 Product at a Time.

With the viability affiliate marketing accomplishes, numerous huge name organizations are currently exploring different avenues regarding it and are discovering achievement. We will propose you start with ClickBank. Start by agreeing to accept a record and pick one product to promote. When you get commissions on somewhere around 5 of the product you are advancing, don't sit down pushing in another specialty or another product.

Pick a product in a specialty that you would appreciate managing. You will compose and inquiring about the hobby and the product. Stick to one product off the start and when you have some accomplishment with it, proceed onward to the following.

The market in just two ways.

There are a large number of products that you can promote, and there are a great many ways that you can encourage them — e-zine, blogging, email marketing, Twitter, YouTube, Facebook, PPC, and so on, and so on.

Stay with two of them to start with, and make them work with one another. For example, on the off chance that you utilize an article catalog, you can have your Twitter account naturally tweet each time you post an article.

Hold on.

Much the same as in any undertaking that you need to make great money in, you should persevere until the point that you make a couple of offers. This may set aside some opportunity to surrender you the heads, yet the reward will be significantly more than justified, despite all the trouble.

In all actuality, there is a significant expectation to absorb information with affiliate marketing and web marketing by and large. In any case, it is one that you can overcome the same number of people have. People that have done it will reveal to you that it genuinely feels like you're procuring money out of nowhere.

Show those that have had immense achievement online and have put the years into it. Never attempt to reevaluate this wheel; be compelling by utilizing the experience of others in this industry. Make a move as quickly as time permits.

How College Students Make Money - Affiliate Marketing

Understudies everywhere around the globe are discovering how undergrads make money over the web using a procedure called affiliate marketing. Affiliate marketing is a type of web marketing which works by the affiliate (which is you) pitching a merchant's product to a client and getting a commission for the deal.

It sounds simple and sufficiently straightforward to do, yet if it were that simple, everybody would do it and profit online. There is sure craftsmanship to having the capacity to make money online utilizing affiliate marketing. How undergrads make money online is by seeing how site design improvement, greeting pages, websites, crush pages and article marketing works.

So you can choose to bounce into Google and type in either "affiliate marketing" or "how undergrads make money online," and I can promise you will have a lot of fun exploring through the minefield of tricks covering the initial 100 pages of Google indexed lists and considerably more after that. There are a lot of methods out there endeavoring to purge understudies' now rare money supply.

Notwithstanding, there are programs out there that are useful and are very to enable you to figure out how affiliate marketing functions and how to make your first couple of offers online, so it's not all fate and melancholy.

The procedure of how understudies make online money functions by investing the exertion. As the colloquialism goes "you just get out what you put in" and that is genuine with regards to affiliate marketing.

In the first couple of weeks, it takes a fair measure of inspiration and drives to get things going and having the capacity to interface how everything functions in your brain. Much the same as at whatever point you are taking in an ability you don't escape, deals from affiliate marketing won't come immediately either.

If a program says that it can make you rich medium-term or it appears to be unrealistic, it frequently is. I propose you start backtracking your means and leaving as quickly as time permits.

How undergrads make money online is by utilizing attempted and tried affiliate marketing strategies that are demonstrated to work time and time once more.

Without a strong base to start your affiliate marketing effort, it will break apart when you begin to start fanning out. This is the reason it is fundamental to get the right aptitudes and preparing so you can set out a firm establishment in which to develop.

How understudies make money online is by creating a solid center establishment in which every single other part and sections of the marketing effort can depend on and fall back on. When you are active with your center battle, you can do this process again in different markets and copy your prosperity.

INSTAGRAM MARKETING, PRO'S AND CON'S

When hoping to get more customers, people swing to online networking. While genuine, a lot of website and business proprietor disregard Instagram as it's a little activity when contrasted and different sites. This is an error, and a smart entrepreneur needs to use Instagram if he or she needs to find more customers. Because of this, there are a few downsides. Here are three experts and three cons of utilizing Instagram.

Stars:

A picture is profitable: As is regularly stated, a view merits a thousand words. Consider it, when running a company, one will need to use images to show off their product or administration. This is particularly imperative when offering sustenance, weight reduction products or whatever other things that people love to take a gander at and appreciate. Be that as it may, one can take it further and show off movement goals or any number of things. Simply put, this is extraordinary compared to other tips for utilizing Instagram for business as a picture will indeed show visitors the accurate estimation of a product or administration.

Viral: Without uncertainty, when utilizing the Internet to advertise a product, administration or thought, one will need it to become a web sensation. On the off chance that a site or thought turns into a web sensation, one will make a lot of money and find a lot of new and energized visitors. Hence, when utilizing Instagram, one needs to make beyond any doubt they provide the excellent incentive to a visitor. At that point, and at precisely that point, one can see the photo become a web sensation, which will result in a lot of new visitors to the site.

They take the necessary steps for the company: Finally, as referenced, when one offers a photo with their friends' et cetera, it can turn into a web sensation. Not just that, when utilizing Instagram, the followers will do the more significant part of the work. Provided a company offers an intriguing photo, it will probably become famous online. At last, one ought to pursue the best tips for utilizing Instagram for business. That way, the followers will do the legwork.

Cons:

More young group: Now, when hoping to find new customers, one will typically need to pursue a more established group. Indeed, while a lot of youngsters and youthful grown-ups use Instagram, not every one of them has the money to spend. Be that as it may, there are opportunities to get them snared and returning when they are more seasoned. In any case, when searching for the best technique for Instagram, one must recollect that not all people can spread out any money.

Not business-disapproved: When following their most loved big name on the web, a lot of people are not inspired by anything but instead squandering inactive time. Which means, while on Instagram, a lot of people are merely hoping to sit back on the train and have no goal of spending any money.

Not household name: While any semblance of Facebook and Twitter are well known, a lot of people don't think about Instagram. This is changing, yet not rapidly, and a smart entrepreneur ought to understand that he or she needs to pursue the best technique for Instagram if they need to find accomplishment as it's not as simple as utilizing other internet based life sites.

When maintaining a website or business, one needs to use Instagram. While not the best amusement around the local area, it's useful to use this web-based life site to find new customers from everywhere throughout the world.

The most effective method to Make Money On Instagram, Make Money Uploading Pictures!

Instagram has turned into the following enormous thing. Users of Facebook are moving toward Instagram because the interface and convenience are way better. You can likewise associate with your fans rather than just friends, and this can be VERY amazing.

On the off chance that you possess a primary Instagram account with a lot of followers you will be viewed as an expert. Whatever you post will be enjoyed and shared. Everybody will label their friends, so their friends can see whatever you transfer. Instagram profiles can get viral, mainly if you are into vines and amusing pictures, or wellness and moving images.

If you at any point pondered whether it's conceivable to make money off of your followers, you are not the only one! With the incredible reaction, there is on Instagram; you can conceivably make many dollars week by week.

If you consolidate commercials alongside your pictures, you will get a lot of activity and conceivably deals. The most vital thing is to avoid spamming and provide usefully related advertisements by your photographs.

As most Instagram users are on their portable, you

should target versatile offers which are visible on a cellphone. Content that doesn't stack on a cell phone won't work by any stretch of the imagination. You should advertise straightforward things, for example, protein powder, wellness types of gear and so forth on the off chance that your page is identified with wellness. You don't need your very own business to offer stuff, as you can fill in as a partner for different business proprietors. They will give you commissions dependent on deals that you provide them. It's honestly as simple as that.

In case you're as of now presently suspecting this won't function as the connections in the picture depiction isn't interactive, you are off-base. The key is to use a URL shortened for whatever product or site you attempt to advance. You can use Bit.ly which is exceptionally prevalent, particularly on Twitter. Or on the other hand, you can use Google's very own shortened: goo.gl. Making little connections will be anything but trying to recall and to type in an internet browser physically.

You can likewise add your connection to your BIO, which makes it interactive. While transferring your picture, you can advise your followers to tap the link in your profile, and they will be diverted directly to your site.

When you have developed a large page you can undoubtedly make money off of it; the most troublesome part is really to build your page. You can ask different Instagramers to shout out your page for you, either for nothing or paid. This will help your record rapidly, and you can increase many followers from a solitary shoutout!

HOW TO MAKE MONEY THROUGH MOBILE MARKETING?

Mobile marketing is a crucial bit of masterminding a business. Anyway, it might be questionable be that as it may! With the various developments, codes, associations, and strategies, it might be shaky to find the right mix for your necessities. Read on to make sense of how you can without quite a bit of a stretch and feasibly facilitate mobile marketing into your business plan.

Make an effort not to send random messages to your customers. Each message you send them should be vital and supportive. You would lean toward not to miss the mark since you send random messages. Customers require quality information from your mobile marketing.

Mobile stages should drive visitors to your main site. Your mobile closeness should be tied in with encouraging people to the home base or remaining in contact with people who were starting at now visit your home base. Never base everything entirely on a mobile marketing campaign.

Customer bases on occasion change yet recall that mobile customers are fundamentally more uncon-ventional due to external effects. This suggests you should screen new releases and remain vanguard on development examples to remain forceful.

Limit the time that you send offers to your customers; nobody needs to get a late night text. Customers will be presumably not going to buy your thing, paying little heed to whether they like it if you have stolen them at odd hours of the day.

Mobile marketing is a remarkable way to make you more profitable. Various people use phones to download distinctive applications, or they use them for long range relational correspondence sites. The two decisions referenced are both unique ways to grandstand your business. Take your marketing closer to where your customers are found.

Giving your mobile marketing advancement watchers an opportunity to provide feedback can empower you to see how your campaign is getting along, and allow you to manufacture customer associations. Customer input is vast, paying little personality to whether it's sure or pessimistic. You should look out customer feedback at each possibility.

Mobile marketing will attract customers; any way you have to make without question it tackles every single mobile gadget. In case the site doesn't work with explicit stages, you are surrendering those potential customers. Do whatever it takes not to leave money on the table over specific issues.

Endeavor two particular pages, called A/B testing, for your mobile page. Director comfort and handiness testing are likewise as necessary for mobile sites concerning the website pages saw through the work zones. Use two extraordinary types of your purpose of entry (known as an and B) to see which one adherent the most. Keep whichever page is more compelling.

In case you are foreseeing sending out text messages, give your audience the decision to choose in and told people how consistently you are going to test them before they join. Text messages can end up chafing given admonitions. Customers may feel angry about the proportion of texts they are tolerating. As such, make without question that only your select in customers get your SMS texts, and never send more than the most extraordinary number of messages decided in the pick in wording. By remaining unwavering to your duties, you will manufacture trust with your customers.

Research about your audience. In case you acknowledge you certainly know their prerequisites, you're undoubtedly going to end up wasting money on your mobile marketing frameworks. Before you spend a penny, choose the tendencies of your potential buyers. It's indispensable to know whether your audience will presumably use their PC or telephone each day. What kind of mobile phone do they use? Find bundles of information about the audience you are trying to target; you will be more viable in reaching them.

When you are mobile marketing based mainly on keeping customers returning, existing customers will most likely distinctly get text messages and constrained time revives. As often as possible, mobile marketing, which is a way for new customers is considered spam.

Mobile messages can genuinely empower you to accomplish your customers when they are moving. As such, to keep all words agreeable to mobile devices grows their capability. Empower customers to click directly on the phone so that they can call you explicitly. Also, make without question that the website that you offer interfaces with show well on mobile devices. A regularly expanding number of people are perusing their email from their phones, and messages should be collected in perspective of this.

Adventure your regular site. A mind-blowing way to move your free spots or phone applications is to pitch them to peruses on your traditional website. That way, customers who make the more significant part of your main site will have the ability to get together with your mobile site as well.

Before you run live with your mobile marketing campaign, make sure to test your notice first. The sending of a message that gets a negative response, or none by any stretch of creative energy, will contrarily influence your campaign. In any case, send it to your teammates to see what they think.

Sending offers, again and again, is bothering and will turn customers off. The best profit will be for the remote possibility that you send out offers wherever from once every week to three times each month. Make a sentiment of sincerity and let your customers understand that powerlessness to act may make them leave behind a considerable measure. In the occasion that you've set them up to expect an impressive proportion of offers in a short timeframe, they likely won't make provoke move.

Underscore the passageway to excellent game plans and the potential hold supports when you are asking for participation in your mobile marketing campaign. Notice it on your website, in advancements, and on various casual associations. In case your audience sees any favorable position in your drive, they will pick in. Present your mobile campaign as an unfathomable way to have a tremendous amount of fun and remain to teach of one of a kind offers.

Think about what your targets are BEFORE you start orchestrating your mobile marketing campaign. You'll need to make a feeling of what exactly you wish to achieve and how you can get that outcome. Your goal may be to extend your business development, pull in repeat customers or to speak with customers.

The best strategy to Make Money Through Automated Forex

Winning advantage and salary has driven both energetic and elderly individuals people alike to search for changed ways and techniques for obtaining money with little theory included. This is a hard truth that can't be denied, especially nowadays wherein the whole world is going up against a money-related crisis. This is particularly clear last 2008 when the world financial superpowers were hit by the worldwide subsidence that cost an expansive number of people their businesses. Helpful thing since there was an industry that didn't persevere through great misfortunes in the midst of such times and that is the business of FOREX or foreign exchange, with the introduction of Automated Forex that various industry objected to people consider today.

Forex or outside exchange incorporates the money of different countries wherever throughout the world, in a perfect world first world and second world countries like the United States, Japan, China, Australia et cetera. The objective of this kind of trade is to buy forex at the most decreased possible expense and after that to offer such forex at the most raised reasonable cost in the midst of a particular timeframe, usually around 3 to 5 business days or even less. By playing the cards right, a forex trader can instantly secure countless with just a single trade. The best part here is that there is as of now the as of late available Automated Forex software that allows a forex trader to screen the events in the forex world thus.

The traditional procedure for physically investigating the examples on the forex publicize is a relic of days passed by. You never again need to devote broaden timeframes of your time to check whether there is any change that may happen that will affect the sudden addition or decay of the expenses of your financial principles. All you require is the automated forex software that can manage predictable seeing of such changes. You can sit back, loosen up and do other also essential things while the forex software does most of the tireless work for you! You have the possibility of getting stores of money and advantage without submitting a significant piece of your time and essentialness at the same time!

Sales Coaching - Discover 4 Steps to Make Money Through Sales Coaching

There is only a single dolt verification way to make money through sales coaching, and that is to get your potential customers to join your coaching programs. Here's the method by which you can do that:

1. Make your one of a kind website. The essential thing that you need to do is to be observable in the online field where you can without a doubt associated with people who require your organizations. Make your very own website and make it say a ton in regards to your inclination in the field of sales and marketing.

2. Desire your visitors to connect with you. You ought to collect an advancing correspondence with your prospects beforehand you can change over them to buying customers. You can do this by asking them to connect with you. Give them an association or a phone number where they can without a lot of a stretch interface with you should they have any request. When you take a couple to get back some self-restraint of them, acknowledge the open way to grant the points of interest that your sales coaching can offer.

3. Summary building. Make without question that you get the contact information of all your web visitors particular the people who are leaving without making the solicitation or making a purchase. Post picks in structures on your website pages and hurls a couple of complimentary blessings. It can undoubtedly enable your join to rate in no time.

4. Improvement. Send your potential buyers with handouts and consider them up all the time to extend their energy over your coaching programs. Each time you do, remember to confer the high ground and offering motivations behind your commitments as these can potentially affect the acquiring decision of your arranged buyers.

CHAPTER FOUR

HOW TO MAKE MONEY OFF A BLOG WITH THE RIGHT MESSAGES

We regularly hear the prosaism "what leaves your mouth is an impression of your identity and character." True enough, the messages you use to pass on your considerations and to persuade others to acknowledge your position play a somewhat primary point for your success. The capacity to make and convey messages that impact understudies, workers, markets, and different types of audiences may appear to be an ability that a few people have while others don't. In this digital age, with the presentation of blogging, realizing how to express one's contemplations can be monetarily gainful for grown-ups as well as for children who need to learn how to make money off a blog.

Regardless of whether you are beginning on a blog or recording an open discourse or communicating a straightforward thought, characterizing your destinations is imperative. Your message has a more noteworthy shot of success on the off chance that you know from the begin what you anticipate accomplish with it. It is safe to say that you are essentially blogging for the sake of entertainment? Is it true that you are attempting to set up yourself as a specialist in your field? Is it true that you are endeavoring to advance your business? Your words must affect, must be correct and reliable, and should contact people. Probably the best discourses are more intuitive than balanced. You realize your message changes when it addresses people's very own encounters.

Another perspective to consider is the amount you know your audience. Think about what your specific audience would need to hear. Is it accurate to say that they are longing for new data or experiences? What issue do they plan to fathom? Give them what they need and need. Your content ought to imitate the desires for your audience. For instance, how to make money off a blog would be decidedly not quite the same as what you would regularly have with business experts, regarding your content and approach. Solicit yourself what kind from the message is this specific audience prepared to hear? Never feel wrong when you foresee any presumptions or misunderstandings that your audience may land at. Thus, it is fundamental that your blogs welcome the audience and welcomes them to participate in a two-manner discussion. By doing this, not exclusively will it demonstrate your audience that you esteem them. However, it will fuel the exchange. It will make them see the amount you value them by including them and remembering them through significant two-route discussions, rather than merely having a restricted monolog.

In like manner, being steady enables you to live up to your audience's desires. Having a key message helps your audience in holding data and should assist in accomplishing that consistency. While you might be enticed to discover engaging approaches to state things, this frequently makes your audience recognize trouble in understanding your true significance. Decide the core of your message and realize how best to build and convey it. Infuse your identity into your words and adjust a positive tone to your conveyance, at that point remain steady with that condition all through.

In conclusion, keep your messages short. There are a few people that basically can't ingest excessively data at a time. As is commonly said, don't give people more than what they can process. Utilizing short, explanatory sentences will add immediacy and clarity to your message.

Building blogs to interest a particular audience isn't an easy procedure. In any case, you should likewise recall that the message and how it is being conveyed is similarly as vital. On the off chance that you have examined your specific audience painstakingly, you ought to have a quick thought of how these people take data in and start to process it. When you have started creating your messages, test them. You may solicit some from your companions or families to be your intended interest group and tune in to your notes, and after that give you criticism.

As should be obvious, having extremely unusual content is only one of the numerous routes on the best way to make money off a blog. Blogging implies getting the chance to discuss your most loved things, composing imaginatively, and in particular, profiting. It takes time, involvement and concentrates on making a luring blog. Your physical market is continually changing, so it just makes sense to keep things liquid. Endeavor to check out you and see what pulls you in.

Instructions to Make Money at Home - Why Online Opportunities Are Goldmine to Be Tapped

If you are considering how to make money at home, going online is undoubtedly the best approach for. It is a goldmine not so much tapped by numerous people. If you need to earn money at home, you ought not to pass up a great opportunity the online opportunities effectively gotten to through the internet.

In this busy current society that we are in now, a great many people are busy with their timetable however not earning enough. In the event that you have an occupation, regardless of whether you put in 24 hours working, you will in any case not gain to such an extent and will understand that when coming to retirement, you don't have much money left in your pocket since all were spend to see through the high living expense.

If you are an understudy, you are so busy with your investigations and extra activities that you scarcely discover enough time for different things. Some may even need to work low maintenance to help themselves through their training which could be a terrible impact for their investigations because of less time spend on their homework.

Concerning people who have effectively resigned, they may have annuities to see them through their life. In any case, the vast majority who left needed extra money to have an actual existence that they can surrender serenely. Tragically they couldn't work any longer, as a large portion of the companies will dismiss them on account of the age. For a few, they may not have annuities to enable them to resign and don't have work to help them. The central arrangement presently is to earn money at home. This is by benefiting the opportunities online.

Regardless of whether you are an understudy who doesn't have room schedule-wise to do extra activities or a retiree who nobody need to utilize you, in the event that you are discovering how to make money at home, you would now be able to take advantage of the a great many opportunities accessible online to earn extra income from the solace of your home. All you need is a PC with a quick internet association.

If you search on the internet, you can discover approaches to make money online. You can make money taking studies, as companies will reward you the time for topping off overview structures to get criticism for their items or administrations. You can earn money at home with information passage occupations which incorporate arranging the companies' databases, planning of the spreadsheet et cetera. In any case, you need to be mindful of making beyond any doubt you work with real companies, as there are numerous tricks out there in the market.

THE BEST ONLINE BEGINNERS TIPS - HOW TO MAKE MONEY NOW

If you are a starter to the online money making the industry, you are likely interested in realizing how to make money now. One of the numerous reasons concerning why a few people are swinging to the internet is its guarantee of producing income rapidly, but you can work for yourself. In any case, what you cannot deny is that online money making opportunities are the equivalent with some other business or earning opportunities that require your time and exertion to manufacture.

Here are a couple of systems that you can utilize on the off chance that you need to learn more on the most proficient method to make money now:

Search Engine Optimization

Getting high search engine results is one of the destinations for upgrading your site so programs and web clients can effortlessly search them. If you are interested in learning how to make money now with your online business, at that point you need to remember what are the elements that could influence your execution in search engine results. They are recorded underneath:

1. Utilizing the correct catchphrases
2. Choose applicable and quality content
3. Improvement of your page catchphrases
4. Make an inbound link technique to drive more activity into your site

Discovering Quality Inbound Links

Making links to your site, regardless of whether inbound or outbound, is significant in deciding the importance of your site. In this way, trade links just with power sites or those that have guide criticalness to your site as a strategy for building your network. On the off chance that you need to realize how to make money now with your online business, this is one of the principal techniques you need to take about, and that is building quality links. How would you do that? Here are factors you need to look carefully:

- Quality of links
- title watchwords
- anchor content
- relevance of the content

Online Money Making Myths

Legend 1: Online money making is like a "pyramid scheme."

While a couple of success accounts of people with profiting online are trying to trust, they are genuine and conceivable. In any case, success in this field (and in some other area, so far as that is concerned) takes time and exertion. If you need to learn how to make money now with your very own online endeavors, at that point you should set aside the opportunity to think about what you need to do to set up a business that will produce the income you need.

The beneficial thing with online money making opportunities is that you can impact the elements that decide the success of your business. For instance, you can execute methodologies to expand movement or construct links that will support the significance of your site. The majority of these endeavors will set aside a specific measure of opportunity to have the capacity to create site visits and manufacture the certainty of your guests as well as for the search engine also to remember you as an expert site.

Fantasy 2: Online income is "easy money."

If you quit your regular employment imagining that taking part in an online business will give you easy money by just sitting throughout the day and trusting that your cash will heap up, at that point you are unquestionably off-base. On the off chance that you need to realize how to make money now using the online business, there are a few opportunities for you to browse. In this way, you need to pick the technique you are most alright with and work on that.

One of the greatest wellsprings of income over the internet is through associate promoting wherein you enable individual companies to offer their item. You can earn commissions from each deal produced through the member program. To learn how to make money now, you need to teach yourself about these different opportunities accessible on the internet and develop on that. Similarly, as with whatever other businesses, the amount you earn will be dictated when and exertion you put into it.

E-COMMERCE: HOW TO MAKE MONEY WITH AN ONLINE SHOPPING STORE.

What is E-business?

Web-based business alludes to a business led online. The most famous example of eCommerce is online shopping, which is characterized as purchasing and selling of products through the web on any gadget.

Web-based business is the quickest developing retail market, and it is assessed to reach over $4 trillion in deals in 2020.

Internet business is a genuinely straightforward yet gainful technique for profiting online, and this guide will center around making an online store utilizing Shopify to offer products.

Beginning

Before you construct your online store, you need to comprehend what to offer and how to source it. Initially you need to discover a specialty, for example, fitness, innovation, bodycon/summer dresses, pet products, and infant products are viral at present.

You can likewise go on Instagram and see what the majority of the favorite Instagrammers are elevating to get a thought of what you should offer. Detox and weight reduction teas and bare-backed, strapless bras and attire appear to be popular.

Another site where you can do some research is Amazon, you take a gander at the bestselling products in a specific class and record them. This trap is outstanding however since you will offer these products all single site and not Amazon you don't need to stress over any immediate rivalry.

At long last, you can go on YouTube and type in "fitness tracker audits," "summer dress survey" or an audit of any product you have found for extra motivation.

Setting up your store: Starting Out

In the wake of doing your research, make a rundown of at least 20 products you need to source, next:

Make an online store with Shopify, it is free for 14 days, and no Visa is required, anyway, amid the preliminary you ought to have sufficiently made deals to kick you off and prop your store up.

You can browse a scope of free and premium subjects to enable you to breathe life into your store.

When you have joined, you can utilize the ground-breaking Oberlo plugin which is accessible through the store manufacturer; this will deal with the putting away and delivering by enabling you to robotize the fulfillment process.

Oberle is an outsourcing plugin which implies that you won't need to store, pack and ship any products physically. You essentially import products from Oberlo into your store and begin selling, the providers do everything else, this is the excellence of outsourcing.

On the off chance that you plan on merely utilizing Oberlin, you can skip "The Finishing Steps (Alibaba)" area after perusing "The Finishing Steps (Oberle)" segment.

Setting up your store: The Finishing Steps (Oberlin)

Next, you need to set up a payment processor on your Shopify store; you can utilize Shopify Payments or an outsider arrangement like PayPal and Stripe.

Make a record on AliExpress and utilize Oberlo's chrome augmentation to import your picked products in no time flat.

Setting up your store: The Finishing Steps (Alibaba)

To start with, set up a payment processor, either Shopify Payments or an outsider processor like PayPal or Stripe, you can see a rundown of upheld payment passages recorded by nation here.

If it's all the same to you fulfilling orders yourself you have some startup cash you can go to Alibaba, look for the products you recorded, find 2– 3 providers, arrange an example, at that point once you are upbeat, you can organize your first batch. It is best to begin with little amounts for your first batch:

- 100– 300pcs for extremely cheap products (not precisely a dollar)
- 100pcs for cheap products ($1—$9)
- 20– 50pcs for costly things ($10 or more)

Delivery doesn't take too long so you can generally top up your starter batch when deals get.

It is best to begin your first batch basic, for example in the event that you are selling fitness trackers, starting with one shading and 50pcs, on the off chance that you are selling dresses, begin with 2– 3 hues in 3 sizes (S, M, L) and 20– 50pcs each.

Your store ought to look great at this point, on the off chance that you need product pictures you can generally request that the providers give you them, this is less demanding than taking the photos yourself.

Marketing: Leverage the Power of Social Media

Presently your store is ready for action, next you need to tell people about your new business! Social media can be an incredible marketing device once you realize how to utilize it.

Facebook Adverts

To run a Facebook Ad crusade, you will initially need to set up an FB page for your business and run two adverts, one to publicize your Facebook page and one to connect back to your store.

Set a financial plan of $6—$10 multi-day relying upon the amount you will spend however ensure you place a final spending plan of £50—$100 altogether.

Concerning on your FB page, present relevant content on the specialty you are selling in, for example, if you are selling fitness products, current articles related on fitness to keep your gathering of people locked in.

The point of your Facebook page is to draw in intrigue

so stay with connecting with, fascinating and even interesting substance as long as it is identified with the specialty your product is selling in.

Instagram Marketing

Keep in mind the Instagram example I referenced before? Well, now you can contact the favorite Instagram influencers yourself and inquire as to whether they will advance your products for you.

Uncovered as a top priority that the bigger after the influencer has, the more they will anticipate that you will pay, the littler and less important influencers may even do a few advancements for nothing to kick them off yet I depend on free promotions as a technique.

Check what number of adherents the influencer has an offer to pay $25—$50 to influencers who have 100,000– 250,000 supporters.

You can even contact Instagrammers with under 100,0000 adherents (i.e., 60,000– 90,000) yet don't offer more than $25 for advancements from them.

When you have discovered your picked Instagrammer, send them a DM and get arranging!

Marketing: Customer Targeting

While targeting your customers, it is best to be particular; this goes for FB advertisements and social media pages.

If you are selling fitness watches, target people who are dynamic and heading off to the exercise center routinely, If that you are selling diet formulas, target people who are attempting to get more fit.

When running your adverts, it regards pick huge urban areas (for example Los Angeles and New York on the off chance that you are targeting US customers and London or Birmingham on the off chance that you are targeting UK based customers).

Wrapping Up

So to entirety everything up:

- Research potential products utilizing Amazon and rundown 20 of your most loved products

- Fabricate your online store with Shopify

- Utilize the Oberlo plugin or source products utilizing Alibaba.

- Setup your payment processor

- Market your store utilizing Facebook and Instagram.

- At long last keep in mind to reinvest your benefits, as your business develops, the request will develop so you need to return your cash to your business to take into account the convergence of new customers.

HOW MUCH MONEY CAN YOU MAKE WITH AN ECOMMERCE STORE

The amount of Money Can You Make With an Ecommerce Store?

The purpose behind this is straightforward; there isn't a limit to the amount of cash which you'll have the capacity to make. It doesn't make a difference whether you're hoping to acquire $10,000+ every month, or you're merely attempting to save up some additional money for a blustery day. For whatever length of time that you're maintaining your e-commerce business effectively you'll have the capacity to achieve whatever financial goals you set for yourself.

We've created this section to demonstrate to you industry standards to begin making sales with your e-commerce business, and we've incorporated some free instruments which you can use to enable you to deal with your accounts. Toward the finish of this part, you'll be filled with e-commerce thoughts to make cash for your store.

How about we begin.

Generating Traffic is Essential for a Successful Ecommerce Store.

It's essential that you're ready to drive a lot of traffic to your online store. At the point when your e-commerce business has an abnormal state of traffic, there are a lot of potential customers who are visiting your store and review your items. If your e-commerce store is selling incredible things at a moderate value point at that point it won't be long before you begin generating both traffic and revenue.

Tragically, there's no assurance that you'll generate traffic to your online store straight away. You'll likely need to exploit marketing channels to draw traffic to your store. Before settling on a choice about which marketing channels are the best fit for your e-commerce business, it's essential that you're mindful of the amount of traffic which you'll need to generate to achieve your financial goals.

Seeing How Much Traffic You Need

The amount of traffic which you'll need to generate for your e-commerce store will contrast contingent upon the amount of cash that you need to acquire.

You can without much of a stretch discover the amount of traffic which you'll need to generate by utilizing Oberlo's Dropshipping Traffic Calculator. All you need to do is input the amount of cash you need to acquire and the number of days you need to take to gain it in. The instrument will separate the number of guests which you need to draw to your online store and the number of requests which you'll need to generate.

Note that the estimations from this precedent accept the following:

• The average conversion rate for an e-commerce business is 2%. This implies for every 100 individuals who visit your store you can anticipate that two individuals will make a request.

• The average requests an incentive for e-commerce stores is $45. This number is taken from Oberlo's client insights.

• You will utilize a 2x edge. This implies you'll be charging your customers twofold the value that you buy the items for.

• The average cost to secure a client is $0.35. This measurement depends on e-commerce businesses utilizing Facebook promotions in the US.

• When you have a comprehension of the amount of traffic which you will need to generate to achieve your financial goals you'll need to consider how you'll make the truck to your online store.

The most effective method to Generate Traffic

The quickest method to generate traffic to your online store is through marketing efforts. There is a wide range of marketing channels which you can use to draw potential customers to your e-commerce store. Each marketing channel has one of a kind advantages and requires a differing level of investment from your side.

We've broken down the distinctive marketing channels which you can use to enable you to make the correct choice for your e-commerce business.

PPC Marketing Channels

PPC marketing, or pay-per-click marketing, involves businesses paying for a superior opportunity to generate traffic for their online stores. If you've ever seen that a Google query item had a yellow 'Advertisement' logo beside it, or a Facebook post with 'Supported' at best, at that point you've just observed PPC marketing in real life. Fruitful e-commerce stores typically have some PPC marketing efforts running, as it's an extraordinary method to make sales.

PPC marketing is extraordinary for generating traffic, expanding mindfulness for your image, and at last, increasing the number of sales you make. You'll receive results from your battles rapidly, and you'll cause marketing charges when someone taps on your advertisement.

There are three fundamental stages which you can use for PPC marketing which are Google, Bing, and Facebook. On the off chance that you pick Google or Bing for your PPC marketing you'll have the capacity to examine the number of individuals who are hunting down what you are posting, which will make your e-commerce stores advertisements more effective. The drawback of utilizing Google and Bing is that you won't have correct data about your intended interest group, similar to their age, sex, or interests.

If you're utilizing Facebook for your PPC marketing, you will have the capacity to acquire data about your group of onlookers' age, sexual orientation, and premiums. However, you don't know how long your advertisements will be.

If you're keen on experimenting with PPC advertising, look at this Google AdWords manage by Neil Patel and Buffer's Facebook Marketing guide for additional data.

Ease Marketing Channels

If the possibility of investing cash into your marketing endeavors sounds like an overwhelming prospect, then you can exploit minimal effort marketing channels. Ease marketing channels take more time to yield results than PPC marketing, so it'll make more time to draw the critical traffic to your online store; however, whenever done effectively they can offer a cost-effective approach to bring traffic to your e-commerce store.

Content marketing is a common ease marketing channel which you can use to generate traffic to your online store. You can make a blog and distribute canny SEO content which is identified with your items to expand your natural hunt rankings and brand specialist. You can utilize internet based life for your eCommerce business to alarm your group of onlookers about new things, streak sales, or declarations identified with your e-commerce store.

There are likewise dialog stages, like Reddit, which you can use to generate more traffic for your online store. Reddit has a wide assortment of particular specialty classifications which are known as 'Subreddits' that you can use to connect with different clients who are keen on your items.

If you've created any substance marketing assets, you can likewise share them on Reddit, giving that they're significant to a progressing talk. As you realize that these clients are occupied with your specialty, it's an incredible method to draw high-potential customers to your online store while making mindfulness for your image.

Working Out Your Profits

At the point when your e-commerce business begins to make sales it's imperative that you can work out the amount of the cash is benefit. Oberlo has created a basic Monthly Profit Calculator on Google Sheets which you can use to work out the amount of benefit that your online store is generating — all you need to utilize it is a Google account.

All you need to do is duplicate the frame which we've created and glued it into your own Google Sheet, and you can enter your very own considers along with the segments set apart in green. When you've input, you consider along with the parts in green the Monthly Traffic Calculator will generate your gross revenue, net revenue, and your benefit. It's critical that you see how the computations for total income, net tax, and gains work, so we've broken them down beneath:

Gross Revenue: You can work out the total income

which your online store has earned by duplicating the value which you're selling your items for by the number of things which you've sold.

Net Revenue: To work out the net revenue you'll first need to duplicate the cost which you secure your items for by the number of items which your online store has sold. When you've finished that whole, you subtract your outcome from the gross revenue, and you'll arrive at your e-commerce business' month to month revenue.

Benefit Earned: To work out the benefit which your store has earned in multi-month you subtract your marketing spending plan from your net revenue.

WHAT IS AMAZON FBA?

An inquiry that is on numerous people's lips is "What Is Amazon FBA"? To enable me to clarify what Amazon FBA is, let us take a gander at a little story, of how Amazon FBA can allow you to make your internet selling business to the following dimension.

Amazon FBA or to give it, it's full name Fulfillment by Amazon is a program set up by Amazon that allows you to utilize Amazon to the warehouse and after that convey your items (and furthermore always you to offer your questions on the Amazon Site). Amazon FBA is exceptionally straightforward, and yet is incredible and can take your business to the following dimension for low costs.

Envision the scene you are occupied with doing your product sourcing and have gotten a few books, CD's DVD's, Home and Beauty items a couple of new toys (Yes items sold through Amazon FBA must be either new or collectible). Presently ordinarily at the back of your mind, you suppose I wish I could buy more stock. However, there is no more space at home. This is the place the Amazon FBA becomes an integral factor. Furthermore, you can only test the water out of utilizing the first Amazon selling account, or you can be a Pro-Merchant, it doesn't make a difference.

You have gotten back home and output or rundown the items as usual into your Amazon selling account and a couple of snaps later, you print out some standardized tags which you should put over the first scanner tag on the item (Yes items should have a standardized ticket or recorded on the Amazon site). A couple of more snaps and you print out a pressing slip which goes in the box or boxes. You at that point book a get from a bearer, and this depends on where you live and how you pay for it - every nation is unique.

Next, you finish the request and trust that the application will be grabbed, and inside days your item will be in the Amazon warehouse being sold for you, and you can kick back and bank the money. Amazon FBA manages installments, delivery, and client messages; you need to source more stock and bank the money.

Indeed, there are some additional costs that Amazon charges yet these are low, and the reserve funds you make on the postage is incredible - recall you are utilizing Amazon's buying power and no more lines in Post Offices and no all the more purchasing air pocket wrap and boxes.

Something different people don't understand is that you can utilize Amazon FBA to dispatch out to your eBay and different buyers. Indeed, Amazon store the items, and send the details out for you. What's more, for next to no cost and by and large much less expensive than you can do. All the valuing data can be found on your nations Amazon site. Just complete a look for Amazon FBA.

The most effective method to Make $10,000+ Per Month With Amazon FBA.

Amazon FBA (Fulfillment By Amazon) is a business opportunity given by Amazon to urge business-proprietors to list their products in its marketplace.

The model works by Amazon furnishing clients with the capacity to send their products to its warehouse and having them "satisfied" by the hold Goliath (it sends them out) upon fruitful buy.

The motivation behind why Amazon would do this is somewhat to get free specialty products which are both remarkable and significant (you claim the products - they merely dispatch them for you), and incompletely to make utilization of their enormous foundation (which they would pay for anyway).

It likewise adds to their offering as a business, as it gives them a significantly more different exhibit of products to add to their portfolio (which is essentially their center upper hand).

The interesting imperative point about the "FBA" demonstrate is that it is characteristic of the new "advanced" business culture that appears to have turned out to be considerably more predominant after the 2008 accident. As opposed to keeping a lot of stock, overheads and a vast group... organizations have taken to the Internet and online networking to discover buyers and make lean endeavors.

Gone are the days when wholesalers decided the destiny of products. Presently, new businesses, business people and regular people can make $10,000+ every month salary streams without owning any land. All the framework, marketing, and satisfaction are dealt with by an entirely independent company (Amazon) - to which you take the necessary steps of sourcing a useful product.

To decide whether you'd get a kick out of the chance to pick up a favorable position from this technique for the venture, I've done this instructional exercise to clarify the way toward using Amazon FBA. Instead of endeavoring to get by on scraps from a nearby market, the new "advanced" domain with all its guarantee is a standout amongst other ways to get your foot in the entryway of the new universe of this business.

How It Works

All businesses work similarly - buy/manufacture a product, offer the product to a market and any "profit" you're ready to make can either be utilized to live off or reinvest into more/better products.

The problem for the vast majority is two-crease:
1) they have no product
2) they have no access to a market.

While both are genuine problems - which would have been a considerable disadvantage in a time without the "advanced" medium - times have proceeded onward to the indicate that obstructions section are low to the point that you just genuinely need to have the capacity to contribute a few $1,000 to have the opportunity of selling to a worldwide gathering of people.

What's more, in spite of the way that the "Amazon" opportunity has existed for right around 10 years now (anybody can list products in its marketplace), the "FBA" display (which is genuinely uninvolved) has just begun to end up well known in the previous two years or somewhere in the vicinity.

If you went poorly business school, to quickly disclose how to run a "fruitful" business, you fundamentally need to be capable give a product/

administration to a vast crowd. You'd typically go for around 30% net profit edge (after COGS and publicizing costs). How you do this is dependent upon you - the key is to buy low, offer high.

Presently, because the "advanced" domain is expansive doesn't mean it's without the way in which "markets" regularly work. The rivalry is power, just like the possibility that since something is "simple," it tends to be generally recreated basically by others (prompting a disintegration of your profits).

Selling on Amazon regularly works by giving access to products which people either don't approach locally, or can get locally however with significant confinements, (for example, shading/measure issues), or with problems inconsistent quality of supply. As it were, while the Amazon marketplace is tremendous - don't figure you can outsmart supply/request.

The good trap with "advanced" businesses is to give access to exceptional products (usually made independent from anyone else or your company) which are just accessible through you. These products must be centered around providing an answer that the vast majority have no clue about, and hence makes the recommendation of buying it through the Internet authentic.

Making an "extraordinary" product is 1,000x simpler said-than-done - the trap with it is to work on answers for your problems. Work towards honing a skillset, which you're ready to apply to a more extensive gathering of people, from which you'll have the capacity to distinguish "products" which can be made and offered as a way to rearrange/take care of problems you've encountered yourself.

Steps

To start selling on Amazon, there are a few stages to take:

The stage no.1 is agree to accept Amazon Seller Account. The first initial step is to get a "dealer" account from Amazon. There are two kinds of vender account - "individual" and "expert." An individual is free and allows you to "list" items which as of now exist in the Amazon inventory. You pay a little expense each time a product is sold. Proficient costs $40/mo, and has no additional "per deal" charges (albeit different expenses, for example, a stocking charge and so forth may apply). This is the primary account which allows you to list new items in Amazon's index.

Agree to accept GS1 This enables you to create barcodes. They come in two arrangements - UPC

(Universal Product Code) and EAN (European Article Number). While these can generally be purchased inexpensively ($10), Amazon, Google, and eBay firmly prescribe utilizing GS1 for institutionalization. By using GS1, you're ready to have your products perceived by any semblance of Amazon. The drawback is the cost. However, it shouldn't generally matter - I always prescribe setting aside ~$500 for administrative costs, of which this would be one.

Make A Legal Company (Optional) If you're hoping to set up a good FBA activity, you'll need a lawful business (and ledger). Aside from enabling Amazon to open a business account, it allows you to all the more likely oversee charges (which are famously terrible for putting your very own money in an individual limit). This is anything but difficult to set up, however, is just fundamental if you need to manage Amazon on an FBA premise as it were real. If you need to offer products on the framework merely, the pleasure is all mine to do it under your very own name.

Buy/Build Boxed Products You at that point need to get a set of boxed variants of the product. If you make the product yourself, you need to get them into traditional boxes. Since there are such vast numbers of ways to do this, we'll say that you should search for a boxing/printing company to deal with it for you. There are numerous able ones. You should likewise follow

Amazon's rules on what sorts of bundling they acknowledge.

Send The Products to Amazon Once you have the boxed products, you need to send them to Amazon. This is organized through the Amazon merchant framework, allowing you to pick a time when the products ought to get at the Amazon warehouse. Once more, because of the dimension of variables simultaneously, it's best to state that you ought to follow the Amazon rules with the end goal to do this.

Begin Selling This is the hardest part, which is clarified below.

Selling The Products

The last advance is to get the products sold. This is the hardest as you're mostly at the impulse of the market (both Amazon's and some other market you may convey to the stage).

The secret to getting products purchased from Amazon is powerful marketing.

Marketing boils down to a few points - the most beautiful being that you need to have the capacity to right off the bat draw in consideration of potential buyers and after that assemble request - giving them the opportunity to buy your product as a way to fulfill that request.

While there are numerous ways to do this, you should recall that in case you will do it viable, you need to have the capacity to go out and market the product autonomously of whether it will be famous on Amazon. The less you need Amazon, the more probable it will be that you'll get people buying through the channel.

-

At long last, we should likewise call attention to that any business you influence must to not be considered pure profit.

Your profit ONLY comes after your different costs have been accounted for, (for example, the genuine products themselves, boxes and marketing). It is a freshman mix-up to believe that the money you get from Amazon will be your "bring home" profit - it's not.

IMPORTANT TIPS ON HOW TO MAKE MONEY SELLING ON AMAZON

Since its origin Amazon has given a platform to individuals, little companies and retailers to sell their products and make ordinary income, anyway, a few people don't realize how to make money selling on Amazon. A portion of the means you can pursue to become a top of the line seller in Amazon are recorded underneath.

Pursue Amazon selling standards and guidelines

In the wake of agreeing to accept a seller account. It is essential to pursue all Amazon tenets and product guidelines to abstain from getting restricted. This guideline can be found in the assistance area of the Amazon site.

Endeavor to be an Amazon highlighted dealer

Getting the opportunity to be an Amazon include shipper is one way of illuminating inquiry of how to make money selling in Amazon. Although Amazon does not say the correct equation on how one becomes a highlighted dealer, one can without much of a stretch join this lofty gathering following a couple of months by having great sales and excellent customer feedback.

Be adaptable on your pricing

Even though everybody's primary point is to make the most extreme profits, it is imperative to have a compelling pricing system. Check the prices of your competitors and guarantee the price contrast edge is justifiable. In the occasion your product gets more orders, you can marginally build the price to boost profits.

Comprehend Amazon costs and fees

The most productive way on the most proficient method to make money selling on Amazon is understanding the fees and costs included. When you purchase a product to sell on Amazon, you need to price it in a way that you will take care of your expense and still make a nice profit.

You can wipe out shipping fees by utilizing Fulfillment by Amazon, FBA which involves sending your products to Amazon who will then deal with the bundling and shipping to customers.

Amazon likewise charges an assortment of fees including selling and referral fees.

Exploit Amazon promoting apparatuses

Amazon has a few promoting apparatuses that can enable your products to get took note. A portion of this devices incorporates Listmania, Likes, and Tags.

Guarantee you have enough products to take care of market demand

Although most sellers begin little, it is prudent to have enough product supply in the occasion you start getting more orders. This guarantees your customers don't search for choices and you increment your income.

Use Amazon seller focal

The ideal way on the best way to make money selling on Amazon is always to use the seller focal reports. These reports causes one examine sells, potential customers and the viability of advancement and advertising.

Instructions to Use The Amazon FBA Platform For Your Multichannel Orders

Amazon.com is the biggest online commercial center, and the platform continues developing. It offers astounding conceivable outcomes for online retail organizations to advertise products to innumerable shoppers. If you are selling on Amazon.com, you are unquestionably going the ideal way. Be that as it may, if you are offering on Amazon, you might miss out on more product sales. It may seem like a testing errand to widen to more frameworks, yet since you are as of now selling on Amazon.com, it will be anything but awkward to use different platforms to support your sales like the Amazon FBA platform.

Amazon.com gives a Multiple Channel Fulfillment (MCF) choice that will enable you to grow to more sales platforms with scarcely any additional costs.

What Is Amazon Multi-Channel Fulfillment?

As the MCF decision satisfies buys from every single other framework, the FBA bolster from Amazon meets your Amazon orders. You can appoint most fulfillment to Amazon. Regardless of whether you sell things up for sale sites, Shopify, any another platform, Amazon will pick and channel products to your customers. You need to pay for shipping and taking care of.

Multi Funnel Fulfillment empowers you to pick the standard, two-day, or 24-hour conveyance, and it computes shipping and conveyance costs relying upon the measure of the thing combined with the selected shipping approach.

If you might want to use Amazon.com MCF, there are a couple of necessities you have to consider. To start with, you must be approved for FBA, and that implies you have charge cards on record with Amazon. Those cards will unquestionably be charged for fulfillment costs, aside from if your seller account has a positive equalization after that MCF fees will be subtracted from your soundness.

You ought to likewise have an expert seller account with Amazon to use MCF which as a rule costs $39. 99 every month, be that as it may, you don't pay for product list charges.

Exploit Amazon's MCF with These guidelines

Amazon's MCF is an excellent methodology for online stores since you use FBA and may adhere to the previously mentioned prerequisites. In any case, there are a few things that may make this better still for you and besides your customers.

Make use of Messaging on Packing Slips

With Amazon MCF, logos and customization are restricted. You can't comprise of customized embeds or pressing slides; you could have specific communications imprinted on the bundling slide. Make a large portion of these exceptional messages to show that you esteem customer's matter of fact and esteem them as customers.

Change Prices Depending on the Platform

One beneficial thing concerning multichannel selling is that you could design prices to support your income. For example, if you are putting forth a product on Amazon, it may require ease to be competitive. That equivalent product on another framework that isn't as competitive thus can cost more.

Put Aside Some Profits

This tip makes marketing prudence wherever you sell products on the web. You never can tell when capricious costs can come up. With MCF, nonetheless, the pricing can be cost-powerful, you may need to pay for things like conveyance and overseeing supplies, and account costs. Regardless of whether you do pass these costs on to customers, it is typically an intelligent thought to have some money set aside for on the off chance that you have an extraordinary thing and need to show it to other product sales channels rapidly.

CHAPTER FIVE

HOW TO BECOME A TOP RATED AMAZON SELLER?

From its humble roots in 1994, Amazon has developed from a little online retailer to end up one of the world's biggest online stores with various people, businesses, and organizations utilizing its stage to offer their products.

A few sellers don't have a clue about the best and productive ways on the most proficient method to make money selling on Amazon. Probably the ideal means to offer your products on Amazon and turn into a top of the line seller are examined beneath

Guarantee You Have Enough Products

Although it is vital to have a couple of products when you begin selling on Amazon, it is critical to have enough products to provide food for interest if individuals like your products and you start getting more orders. These guarantees return customers, and the individuals who have been alluded don't search for elective sellers.

Your Products Should Be Affordable with Flexible Pricing

The ideal way on the best way to make money selling on Amazon is by selling your products at moderate rates. Check your rival's costs and modify likewise. Although this probably won't get you a sizeable overall revenue at first, it is the ideal way to get and hold more customers.

Moreover, you ought to be adaptable in evaluating. On the off chance that you are the leading seller of a given product and there is expanded interest, you can somewhat push the costs up to build productivity.

Use Amazon Marketing Tools and Amazon Seller Central

Another way on the best way to make money selling on Amazon is by using existing Amazon advertising devices including Tags, Listmania and Likes which will enable your products to get greater permeability. Moreover, Amazon seller central gives ordinary reports that can allow you to dissect your offers, know potential customers and discover the viability of your showcasing and advancements.

Turn into an Amazon Featured Merchant

Being a featured merchant on Amazon won't just get your products saw, yet will likewise make you trustworthy and trusted among potential customers? Although Amazon does not say how sellers end up featured merchant, you can without much of a stretch get to that rundown by having good sales, next to zero customer grumblings and superb customer audits. You ought to likewise guarantee that you cling to all Amazon selling tenets, directions, and arrangements to abstain from getting restricted.

See all costs and fees

The best and proficient way on the best way to make money selling on Amazon is by seeing all related fees and costs. If you are a seller who purchases products, offers them on Amazon, your selling cost must have the capacity to suit every one of your expenses and Amazon fees. Amazon charges fees for selling and referrals

You can diminish your transportation costs by utilizing FBA (Fulfillment by Amazon) where you send your products to them, and they handle bundling and dispatching to customers.

FBA - Fulfillment by Amazon

You may have found out about FBA on numerous sites, particularly on Amazon. FBA remains for Fulfillment by Amazon. What is it and how can it function? Would you be able to set aside extra cash or appreciate different benefits with this offer or process?

FBA is a procedure through which Amazon keeps a supply of a seller's goods and after that rundown them on their site available to be purchased. Besides this, the organization gets installments for each order put on the web, and the conveys the expected goods to every buyer.

With the assistance of this procedure, a considerable measure of stores has delighted in a good deal of development in their sales. A few stores have Amazon finish the orders for goods. Regularly, the products are explicitly sent to the buyers by the sellers selling straightforwardly on Amazon. Now and again, it occurs by the sellers on different sites, for example, Etsy, eBay that moves to the FBA. Along these lines, it's intriguing to know how this offer by the vast store has profited individuals everywhere throughout the world.

As per numerous sellers, they have encountered a remarkable ascent in their sales volume. Then again, buyers trust that they are buying from a commendable trust organization rather than a person. As it were, purchasing straightforwardly using FBA adds to the trust of the buyer in the provider. Thus, they may buy again not far off.

Beside this, sellers can make use of this offer with the end goal to accomplish numerous different benefits. If you use this administration as a seller, you won't need to stress over the advancement of the product. Besides, it will be Amazon's duty to deal with buyers and satisfy orders. Then again, you can center around different undertakings, for example, getting new products and do different assignments that may make your business much higher.

Extra benefits:

If you are a product proprietor, you can take some days off without stressing over who will deal with your business while you are away. Your business will continue running while you are having an incredible time with your companions in Paris. Along these lines, you can avoid your office for the same number of days as you need. For whatever length of time that Amazon has your products in their stock, you are good to go, and you don't have to stress over anything.

A few people don't care to deal with buyers straightforwardly. They think that it's difficult to deal with troublesome customers. Dealing with pressure isn't some tea. These things will be taken care of by Amazon.

If you don't know anything about FBA yet, realize that figuring out how to use it isn't hard in any way. You can go to the official site of Amazon to download the pdf reports to find out about how to begin. In a few minutes, you will be comfortable with the entire framework.

HOW TO MAKE MONEY USING KINDLE PUBLISHING

Kindle self-publishing has given digital book authors new conceivable outcomes to procure a pay. Amazon's electronic ebook peruser is effectively the most well-known one, which implies that the Kindle ebook publishing choice is surprisingly fulfilling.

Some uncomplicated strategies will enable you to win money with Kindle do it without anyone else's help publishing. You can depend on different fundamental tips to enhance the prevalence of your books and furthermore to raise income. Kindle does it without anyone's help publishing: You Need a Great Product!

To make money with Kindle self-publishing, you will initially need to assemble a predominant ebook. Individuals who have an enthusiasm for ebook buys have a considerable number of choices to pick among. An elegantly composed, professionally made ebook is the first opportunity to be discernible.

Examine the topics you know and the things that you appreciate. Your aptitudes will wind up evident in the main pages of the book. Cease from beginning an exceptionally yearning project that you're fresh out of the plastic new to, even though you presume that the subject has important adaptation potential outcomes.

In conclusion, for the prosperous Kindle self-publishing, you ought to rely on master altering. There isn't an option if you wish to change ebook publishing into a profitable private company.

Kindle Does It Yourself Publishing: A Picture Is Worth A Thousand Words!

You have a couple of moments to inspire Amazon customers. A decent ebook cover and a keenly written layout will give you a chance to be discernible. Here's your one opportunity to catch the eye of the group of onlookers with the end goal to create item deals.

Proficient, fascinating and vital cover structures are the underlying thing dealers take note. Bunches of individuals make acquiring choices based on visuals. Having a cover without anyone else is fine if you have picture altering information. Using fantastic photographs and interesting typefaces can enable you to assemble an in vogue cover.

The write-up on the ebook should stress you are essential focuses. Together with some lines of constructive surveys will build up some believability and besides increment the status of people to buy.

Drive Traffic to Your Kindle Self Publishing E-book Web Page

To create pay through Amazon Kindle publishing, you should complete a great deal of publicizing and marketing. The web presents incredible, sans cost attention likely outcomes. Rely on those to push movement towards your Amazon ebook portrayal pages.

Long range interpersonal communication is among the numerous methodologies to show signs of improvement at. Begin a site or even a blog and devote it to the subjects talked about in your electronic books? Include a hyperlink to your Amazon URL in your email signature and furthermore on your independent company card. Pretty much all marketing chances should be utilized expertly and capable of raising benefits and incrementing your Amazon Kindle ebook publishing achievement.

Probably the best Amazon ebook authors create a great deal of money through the work they do. The working of reasonable income is achievable by anybody. You need a brilliant idea and a smart promoting and marketing plan. Investing some energy in the starter steps will enable you to make a captivating electronic book which has a free income building likely outcomes.

Money From Your Camera - Tips to Make Money From Self-Publishing Photo Books

If you felt that the time of advanced with the entry of PDAs and the Kindle would kill off paper publishing, at that point you are off-base. The market is enormous and more books than any time in recent memory are being distributed. Just investigate the racks of your nearby bookshop and see all the new distributions. Here is a market that is just sitting tight for new picture takers.

The book publishing market is extremely rewarding however somewhat hard to enter. With the end goal to get a commission from a publisher, you need to have a portfolio and a reputation. So appears to have shot this idea down on fire, or has it? Try not to be down and out the time of computerized offers another arrangement which is ideal for the sprouting book picture taker. The idea is called print on interest self-publishing. There are such vast numbers of new self-publishing organizations that will print from single duplicates as far as possible up to thousands.

This is energizing yet how would you do it?

1. Research your publisher

The least demanding approach to begin is with Google. Look for print on interest and self-publishing books, and you will find many potential publishers. Be that as it may, don't stop after perusing only the first page on your internet searcher. Prop up for great deals further on take careful note of least amounts and how their framework works.

2. Research your substance

Please find some great deals yet shouldn't something be said about your book? The appropriate response is necessary, most self-publishing organizations add to their arrangements by including additional items like the format, cover plan and altering for nothing or with ease while some add marketing bundles to the deal. In any case, first you need to get the idea together, and the fundamental design of your photographs in the book along with the content or articles you will compose or have written. You need to drive the project since it's your vision and no one will get energized for you.

3. Drive the procedure

Happens when self-publishing that you turn into the general proofreader and as opposed to having the staff to take every necessary step, you are presently paying the self-publishing company. Make beyond any doubt that you have decent learning of what their job will be and what desires you can put on them. Prop the procedure up and make inquiries regularly. If you have a due date, make beyond any doubt it's in the assertion you will at first sign.

4. Who will market the book?

Key to this procedure is finding out what the company's job will be in the marketing of your book which is essential to the overall accomplishment of the project. A significant number of these organizations have online stores yet additionally will complete a restricted measure of marketing and public statements to bookshops and online stores. Be that as it may, you likely find again that you should drive the procedure on the off chance that it is true will be a win. Concoct your very own marketing plan notwithstanding what they will do. Nobody will think about your infant like you so don't expect more than you will give.

5. A foot in the entryway

What a fruitful project like this will accomplish for you is to give you a foot in the entryway and a CV for moving toward potential publishers for future book projects. A decent quality generation will provide a publisher with an idea of what you can convey.

So here's a plan of action:

a. Make the idea or idea for your book. b. Select the photographs and plan all the content or articles. c. Research a self-publisher and choose who to approach. d. Approach a publisher with your idea and a plan of action. e. Present your work and keep close correspondence with your publisher. f. Begin a marketing effort to circulate your books notwithstanding the self-publishing company's offer.

Any photography adventure is continually going to require some serious energy and exertion. You will endure dismissal, and there will be times when you figure it will never work out. Hold tight because determination will dependably satisfy at last if the nature of your work is of a particular requirement.

MAKE MONEY WRITING FICTION BOOKS - 3 STEPS TO FICTION WRITING SUCCESS

Ever thought about how to make money writing fiction? It's a joint inquiry. When you find out about the large number of dollars that numerous top rated authors procure, it's normal to consider how you can transform your adoration for storytelling into a profitable endeavor.

In this section, we'll cover three fundamental advances you'll need to pursue in case you're not kidding about making money writing fiction. Executing these tips isn't simple, yet in case you're willing to invest the energy and exertion, you can accomplish your fantasies.

1) Write a convincing story in a favorite genre.

Being generously compensated for your fiction writing endeavors starts with making a connecting with the story in a favorite genre. This may seem like essential counsel, yet many would-be authors routinely disregard it.

Try not to write a fictionalized story about your life. Try not to write in a genre that hasn't been popular in more than fifty years. Of course, you may be sufficiently splendid to find accomplishment by slighting both of these proposals. However, the chances are against you.

Concentrate the national smash hit records and search for patterns. Select a genre that you appreciate perusing in your recreation time. This is the place you should make your stand.

2) Get a decent abstract agent.

Finding a decent agent is about as troublesome as getting a major publisher, yet it's essential. An artistic agent will market you and your novel to editors and help you get the ideal deal.

Where could you find these people? Look on the web. Go to writer's gatherings. Approach distributed authors for proposals.

Whatever course you pick, remember this: the ideal approach to arrive an agent is to write a convincing, marketable novel.

3) Secure a contract with a major publisher.

In our current period of independently publishing on the Internet, many would-be writers evade the important errand of getting a deal with a big deal publisher. While self-pubbing has its favorable circumstances, much of the time, you'll make significantly more money writing fiction by anchoring a customary book contract that pays a development, and eminences.

How would you get such a contract? Sign with a respectable artistic agent.

Which leads us back to the first tip: writing a marketable novel that readers can't put down.

How to Make Money with Kindle (Kindle Secrets)

If you are a pure blue fiction or right to life author, you can make money with Kindle. Amazon detailed that in December 2011 alone, more than 1,000,000 Kindles were offering every week. Furthermore, that is only a glimpse of a more significant problem. Anybody that possesses a PC, Mac or PC, a tablet, a cell phone or some other electronic gadget fit for joining to the Internet, can arrange digital books from Amazon without having a Kindle.

Kindle Publishing

Publishing on Kindle is available to most anybody, as long as you pursue the tenets. To make money with Kindle, you must know your market, value your books inside their range and market your books. None of that is hard, yet it takes some exploration and some devoted work on your part.

Pursue the Rules

Kindle does not permit member interfaces in books. On the off chance that you put these connections in your books, your books will be pulled. Presently numerous people believe that they can just put "poop" up on Kindle and offer it. While you may offer a couple of horrible things, entirely soon that won't work. The reason? People aren't dumb. They would prefer not to be "sold" to - on the off chance that you give your readership what it needs, you will never lose. Give legit answers for their issues through self-improvement or how-to book, or find an approach to engage them with your fiction. This is a real business try and should be treated like this.

Quality

Give quality books to your readers. Records overflowing with blunders will kill your readers. The general purpose of giving people things to peruse is to provide them with quality artistry, essential data - in case you're giving them self-improvement or how-to sort of book. Give them extraordinary amusement on the off chance that you are writing fiction.

Book Ideas

Stay with contemporary thoughts or go onto to Amazon and look what's offering in the Kindle market. Visit the websites of the authors who appear to make a lot of offers and pursue their leads. Do they distribute week by week to their site? Do they have an email list? Audit their sites and note what you like and don't care for.

Cut Out Your Niche

Cutting out your unique specialty is vital. Try not to having a go at writing over a wide range. Adhere to a specific class, and you'll do well. Abstain from attempting to be everything to all people, find your "clan," your "market," and pull out all the stops. Build up a profile of your regular clients and write articles to address their worries and place them on websites like these. While you can't interface back to your Amazon page, you can connect to your site where you offer your book. Set aside the opportunity to break down your market and this will make a distinction over the long haul. If you finish, you can make money with Kindle.

MAKING SENSE OF SELF-PUBLISHING TERMS

Most authors long for being distributed by a traditional publisher-one who pays to print the author's book and after that pays the author royalties. Notwithstanding, after months or long stretches of mailing out original copies to publishers and artistic operators, and heaps of dismissal letters later-if even sufficiently fortunate to get a reaction to numerous authors at last swing to self-publishing.

At the point when self-publishing is first considered, the author finds that homework is required to comprehend the self-publishing industry. Different websites and Internet gatherings about self-publishing will offer counsel or critique about avoiding POD publishers or subsidy publishers, or about the marks of shame or entanglements of self-publishing. These terms are utilized broadly and conversely and can be confounding to new authors. Here are a couple of fundamental definitions to enable authors to see precisely what these terms mean and a breakdown of what is extremely required to self-distribute a book.

Traditional Publishing: As expressed over, a traditional publisher will deal with all the publishing and printing costs of the book. Authors will receive royalties for their book's deals. All through the twentieth century, traditional publishing was seen as the perfect circumstance for authors because traditional publishers have been seen as the guardians or judges of whether a book is deserving of production. Additionally, traditional publishers would showcase the books and authors had no hazard engaged with the publishing costs.

Changes in the commercial center, notwithstanding, have made it more troublesome for traditional publishers to contend, and by expansion, it is more annoying for authors to be chosen for production. While conventional publishing still gives a specific feeling of authenticity, self-publishing is a more practical choice for most authors, and as a rule, it can likewise be more worthwhile.

Self-Publishing: Self-publishing implies, for the most part, that the author publishes the book himself, and he ingests the cost of printing the book. The preferred standpoint is that the author receives all the benefit, however the weakness is that self-publishing has a disgrace, to a great extent in light of the fact that numerous authors have self-distributed low-quality books that couldn't contend with traditionally distributed books for a number of reasons from modest paper and low-quality printing to various mistakes.

Self-publishing itself has its degrees of what many think about true self-publishing. An authentic self-distributed book, in numerous individuals' conclusions, is where the author supervised the whole creation from design to printing and where the author claims the ISBN, printing the book under his or his very own publishing company's name. While "vanity," "subsidy," and "POD" are terms regularly utilized in connection to self-publishing, they are more similar to relatives of self-publishing because another publisher other than the author is included even though the author fronts the costs.

It ought to be noticed, that traditional publishing has just been the predominant type of publishing in the twentieth century, and it is ending up progressively less prevailing in the twenty-first century. In the nineteenth century, most traditional publishers were littler, some inherently being connected to bookstores. Numerous authors, for example, Mark Twain, Walt Whitman, and Ralph Waldo Emerson self-distributed their books.

Vanity Press: A vanity press is a publisher whom the author pays to distribute his book. In the late twentieth century, loathsomeness stories were regularly told about authors who lost their life-reserve funds by paying a vanity press $50,000 or some other stunning add up to distribute a book, to have the book sell only a couple of duplicates. Choosing to self-distribute by paying a vanity press was a genuine hazard on account of the cost of publishing and an essential motivation behind why most authors looked for traditional publishers. Moreover, the name proposes that the author was vain-trusting his work was meriting production notwithstanding when the conventional publishers dismissed his book. The term is infrequently utilized any more, to a great extent because different words have come into use that better mirror the adjustments in publishing innovation, which has brought about self-publishing costs diminishing altogether.

Subsidy Press: A vanity press and subsidy press might be compatible terms. The thing that matters is that the term subsidy is all the more generally utilized now since it has less disgrace. The author still pays the press to distribute his book, however in the twenty-first century, the cost of publishing a book has dropped substantially because of digital or POD printing.

POD (Print-On-Demand): The self-publishing world much of the time alludes to POD publishers or companies, and it utilizes the term to signify "self-publishing companies" yet POD signifies "print-on-request." Due to new printing innovation computerized printing-it is quicker and more cost-viable to print a book. Up to this point, books were spread out with moveable type, and the procedure was arduous, tedious, and costly, and thusly, just substantial print runs were made on the grounds that it would have been ludicrous to put in the hours or days required to set up the moveable type to print just a single book. Present day PCs in the advanced age, be that as it may, now take into consideration "print-on-request" which necessarily implies on the off chance that somebody needs one book, it tends to be printed promptly. The outcome is that printing is less expensive and quicker. A significant number of the littler traditional publishers utilize POD.

POD Publishers or Companies: Most references to POD Publishers, other than implying that these companies utilize Print-On-Demand or computerized printing innovation, indicate that these are bigger self-publishing companies that an author can pay to deal with all parts of book creation. These companies are moderately cost-compelling. Bundles to distribute a book can keep running under $1,000, which incorporates all elements of structure and format and generally few printed duplicates, for example, 10-50. The author at that point buys copies of his books from the POD company, and the more copies he arranges, the less he pays. The thing that matters is that these POD companies still increase the cost of printing the books to make a benefit. They make their cash selling books to authors, not in selling the author's books to general society. They still frequently work reasonably like traditional publishers, in any case, since they will sell duplicates straightforwardly to bookstores or book wholesalers, for example, Amazon and Barnes and Noble, or Ingram's; these book deals result in eminence checks to the author. POD companies will likewise give their ISBN and distribute the book under their name as opposed to the author's very own publishing company's name. Such companies, as expressed above, resemble stepsisters to both traditional publishing and self-publishing since they blend a tad bit of the two universes.

Co-Publishing Companies: Because of the high costs of publishing, some littler traditional publishers offer co-publishing. Of course, the traditional publisher will deal with all the publishing and printing costs of the book and authors will receive royalties for their book's deals. In any case, the author is requested to buy, e.g., 500 duplicates of the book.

Genuine Self-Publishing: Finally, for those dwelling on silly trifles about evident self-publishing, the author who self-publishes will exclusively contract with (ideally) a manager, somebody to do format, inside and cover structure, and a different printer. For this situation, the author publishes the book with his very own publishing company name he has made for himself, and he independently pays every single substance printer, cover structure individual, inside planner, editorial manager. The author likewise buys his very own ISBN and hence has the book enrolled as being distributed by his very own company. While this type of self-publishing is more work, and it will most likely cost an author more cash forthright than utilizing a POD company, the author will have the capacity to print a more significant number of books for less per unit (singular book), and the author will likewise have the ability to have more power over a definitive look of the book instead of depending on a POD company, which may utilize all the more an essential format way to deal with how the book looks.

Which to Choose?

Eventually, each author must pick which type of self-publishing is best for him or her. To go the straight highway, a POD Company may regard get your feet wet, and after that, as you turn out to be more educated, you can try different things with genuine self-publishing by directing all parts of the production. APOD Company might be perfect for a little print run, for example, 100 duplicates for a book you don't plan to sell or don't think will sell well, for example, publishing Grandpa's diaries or a family parentage that just a little gathering of individuals will need, or a book for an explicit company or association. For a novel or verifiable book with a more extensive collection of people, a specific self-publishing procedure may be an excellent decision. Authors primarily should gauge the benefits of the two types of self-publishing to determine which is best for his or her extraordinary book.

CONCLUSION

Everybody could do with a couple of additional dollars every month, couldn't they? A standout amongst other ways you can do this is by searching for passive income ideas. There are a few ways you can procure passive income on the web yet you need to get into the right programs. Niche affiliate programs are one such zone you should think about because once you do the underlying work in setting up a site and showcasing it, you can kick back and let it do its job-creating passive income for you. It is truly outstanding and most straightforward passive income ideas. Then again, you should think about something like Cagora, a social and community network. The measure of work required here is to a great extent up to you, however, the more people you allude, the happier you are. There is no prerequisite to purchase anything yourself in any case. You procure commission however on any buy from Cagora that any of the people you have alluded make. This is one of the better passive income ideas as the commissions are payable forever, not only a couple of buys. You do need to acknowledge anyway that there is no such thing as a free lunch independent of what you do. Any of the passive income ideas you may require some contribution from you eventually in time whether it be by setting up a web page, offering something straightforwardly or by implication or alluding another person to something. Apologies, yet this is this present reality, and you don't get cash in vain. In any case, you can set yourself up to acquire residual income where the arrival for exertion is low. The best thing about creating passive income online is that you can develop it to the point where it can supplant an all day job. This is definitive you need to achieve where you can appreciate the advantages of working at home with your family. Moreover, in these times of dubious financial times, you can take control of your own life and your income without being in danger of the feared redundancy package. In the case of nothing else, when you are utilized in a job, this would need to be a standout amongst the most convincing motivation to go looking for passive income opportunities. Along these lines, to outline, there are a significant number of passive income opportunities out there. You need to do your due persistence on them and ensure they are a solid match for you and something you will appreciate working to produce the passive income. Good fortunes in investigating all the passive income ideas on the web.

www.ingramcontent.com/pod-product-compliance
Lightning Source LLC
Chambersburg PA
CBHW071652210326
41597CB00017B/2189